THE WRITE THING

KWAME ALEXANDER

ENGAGES STUDENTS IN WRITING WORKSHOP

(AND YOU CAN TOO!)

Kwame Alexander

Foreword by Kylene Beers, Ed.D.

D0874256

Contributing Authors

Chris Colderley, *Teacher, Ontario, Canada*
Ann Marie Stephens, *Teacher, Manassas City Public Schools, Virginia*

Publishing Credits

Corinne Burton, M.A.Ed., *Publisher*
Conni Medina, M.A.Ed., *Managing Editor*
Emily R. Smith, M.A.Ed., *Content Director*
Véronique Bos, *Creative Director*
Shaun N. Bernadou, *Art Director*
Stephanie Bernard, *Associate Editor*
Regina Frank, *Graphic Designer*

For Lois Bridges, educator, publisher, literacy champion,
word whisperer, dream maker, friend, Somethin' Else

© 2019 KA Productions, LLC
All rights reserved.

Shell Education

5301 Oceanus Drive
Huntington Beach, CA 92649-1030
www.tcmpub.com/shell-education
ISBN 978-1-4938-8842-9

The classroom teacher may reproduce copies of materials in this book for classroom use only. The reproduction of any part for an entire school or school system is strictly prohibited. No part of this publication may be transmitted, stored, or recorded in any form without written permission from the publisher.

Website addresses included in this book are public domain and may be subject to changes or alterations of content after publication of this product. Shell Educational Publishing does not take responsibility for the future accuracy or relevance and appropriateness of website addresses included in this book. Please contact the company if you come across any inappropriate or inaccurate website addresses, and they will be corrected in product reprints.

All companies and products mentioned in this book are registered trademarks of their respective owners and are used in this book strictly for editorial purposes. No commercial claim to their use is made by the author or the publisher.

Table of Contents

Part I: Writing

Part 2: Publishing

Part 3: Presenting

Appendixes

Acknowledgments

I liken the process of developing and fine-tuning the writing workshop to jazz. Sure, I'm the bandleader, but the literary magic that's been created on elementary, middle, and high school stages over the past 25 years of my literacy work is the product of an orchestra of writers, educators, librarians, and literacy advocates jamming to the same mission: Getting young people excited about, and engaged with, writing.

Since the inception of my Book-in-a-Day writing and publishing workshops, on which *The Write Thing* is largely based, I've planned, perfected, and riffed on processes and implementation with a wonderful community of working writers and artists. There was certainly planning, but I've always been a believer, like Miles Davis, "that you don't play what's there, you play what's not there." And, so in most of my workshops, in the quest to find the write groove, spontaneity has always trumped planning. Thanks to the talent, trust, insight, and creative energy of my poetry and Book-in-a-Day colleagues—Tinesha Davis, Deanna Nikaido, Janice Sapigao, Joanna Crowell, Ruby Veridiano, Angel Wood, and Titilayo Ngwenya (who, fittingly, happens to be an accomplished jazz singer)— thousands of students have discovered and shared their powerful voices.

T. S. Eliot said, "Immature poets imitate, mature poets steal." While I am proud of the uniqueness of the Book-in-a-Day workshop, I also know that it did not come out of a vacuum. My first formal writing workshop was at Virginia Tech, at the feet of world-renowned poet, Nikki Giovanni. She created an exciting, authentic, and relatable literary environment that I still mimic to this day. If, like Wynton Marsalis says, "a musician's whole life is to listen," then it is the job of any worthy writer to read. At the beginning of my writerly career, as I was trying to translate my love of poetry and literature into a classroom strategy, it was the groundbreaking literacy research and publications of Lucy Calkins, Ralph Fletcher, and the America's Choice Educational Team that provided me with an instructional design model to articulate my goals. The scholarship, activism, writing, and friendship of colleagues such as Pam Allyn of LitWorld, Naomi Shihab Nye, Marshall Johnson, Angela Turnbull,

Toni Blackman, Dr. Marcelle Haddix, and Dr. Bryan Ripley Crandall of the National Writing Project continue to be a source of inspiration and innovative thinking around global and local literacies.

If you've ever heard Cannonball Adderley's stunning 1958 recording of the Miles Davis composition "Somethin' Else," then you know that his playing sounds so smooth, so effortless, it seems, as jazz critic A. B. Spellman has stated, that "he wasn't even paying attention to what he was doing." The tune is magical, and a big part of the reason is that he featured Miles Davis on the record and Art Blakey was featured on drums, and that's a band you don't mess around with. I am thankful to the marvelous musicians who play so perfectly on these pages: Ann Marie Stephens, Van G. Garrett, and, especially Chris Colderley. Chris is a poet, researcher, and elementary school teacher in Hamilton, Ontario, who asked me to bring Book-in-a-Day to his fourth-grade class, and again, up for the challenge, I said yes to our first elementary cohort. It was so successful that we came back four more times, empowering more than 300 student authors of five anthologies. Chris was invaluable in helping me conceptualize this book, and he provided valuable research and editorial assistance that helped round out this text and bring the stage to the page. Andrea Davis Pinkney, Ray Coutu, Sarah Longhi, Brian LaRossa, Danny Miller, Sarah Morrow, Kevin Carlson, and literacy visionary Lois Bridges were guiding lights with a professional touch matched only by their encouragement and brilliance.

I am grateful to all the students and educators who've allowed me to teach (and be taught) during this enlightening journey, especially Noni Carter, Jennifer Brown, Carlin Pierce, Gwen Benton, Nick Grzeda, Mary Pelicano, Gregory David, Priya Sitaraman, Allie Bruce, Linda Holtslander, Dana Davidson, and especially Kim Hardwick, who had the vision for this book long before I did and who has the distinction of bringing Book-in-a-Day to her schools the most times: nine.

Finally, I am indebted to my patient and loving family that continues to share me with the page and the stage: my wife Stephanie, my daughters, Nandi and Samayah, and my parents, Dr. E. Curtis and Barbara Alexander.

Discovering the Neglected Genre

by Kylene Beers, Ed.D.

An old Welsh saying reminds us that there are three things for which we should give thanks: an invitation, a gift, and a warning. Over the years, this adage has sprung to mind when someone has handed me a gift, sent me an invitation, or occasionally offered a warning. And these words came to mind when I received a copy of this book you now hold in your hands.

This book is an invitation. In a time in which education is too often about the correctly bubbled test item, this book reminds us that a true education is far more. Education is exploration of our very selves, our discovery of who we are and where we fit; it's certainly about finding out, but it's also about wondering and wandering. It's about imagining and inventing. It's about where we've been, where we are, and most certainly where it is we might go next. All of that is in this book as Kwame Alexander shows us how to connect children to a genre that is all too often relegated to one month or one unit.

Poetry—what I'll call the *neglected genre*—draws us into ourselves as it simultaneously lets us give back to the world a fresh understanding, a new vision, a re-vision of one moment. Kwame puts it better when he explains that poetry lets us "write our own journeys, find our own voices." Without a doubt, this book invites you on a journey, a process, a discovery of how to connect your students to a genre that encourages creativity and yet honors discipline; that demands imagination, yet is grounded in truth. If you want your focus on poetry to extend beyond the occasionally read poem and if you believe all students have within them that desire to share their truest feelings, then this book is your invitation to change. To connect. To bring poetry into your students' lives.

And perhaps that is what makes this book a gift. First, it's a gift that Kwame has given all of us as he shares his journey, as he shares his voice, as he shares his insights and understandings. As I read the pages, I understood a writer I've always admired has given us all a gift of inspiration and education. His calm you-can-do-this voice rings through these pages and his of-course-you'll-want-to-do-this excitement soars. He tells us that poetry ... *has the power to reach students, tap into their emotional intelligence while allowing them to freely and openly express themselves. It can be the school where our children go in order to learn to write well.*

And then he gives us the gift of showing how to make that happen. In step-by-step specificity, *The Write Thing* shows us how to move students from ideas, to drafts, to finished products, to a published work.

And this book is a gift that we're not expected to keep to ourselves. With videos and mentor texts, Kwame shows us how to share excitement for writing with our students. For those of us who would quickly say, "But I'm not a poet," this book shows us how to unleash the poet Kwame believes resides in each of us, polish our work, and then publish it for an audience—even a small one—so we all see that our poems become a gift to others.

Finally, I'll add my own warning. This book demands your time. It demands your attention. It demands that you examine what you have done and what it is you could be doing. It gently urges you to examine practices and ask yourself (as I had to ask myself), "Do I really understand the power of the poem?" The book is divided into three parts—writing, publishing, and presenting—and concludes with the most helpful Appendix I've ever seen in a book. While it reads fast, this book should not be a fast read. Linger. Muse. Reread. Mark. Read the poems aloud. Write your own poems. Journey into yourself, back into the world, then into your classroom. Share with your kids. And then watch them soar.

An Unconventional, Uncommon Writing Workshop

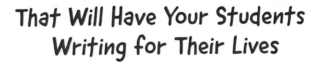

That Will Have Your Students Writing for Their Lives

When I was in college, I wanted to be an actor and a playwright. I'd written a play my sophomore year at Virginia Tech, produced it, and received rave reviews from students and teachers alike. On a dare, I applied to a theater master class, taught by some of the most renowned artists and writers in the industry: Cicely Tyson, Spike Lee, and Charles Fuller. Luckily, I was accepted.

Mr. Fuller, who had just penned the powerful and critically acclaimed film *A Soldier's Story*, starring Denzel Washington, based on his Pulitzer Prize–winning play, led the playwriting component of the class.

We each had to share our work-in-progress, and I remember him telling me that mine lacked soul, it lacked emotion, and while I may have employed some of the devices that make for a good dramatic play, my piece simply was too long and uninteresting. "Go write some poetry," he said. "Poems are the basic building blocks of all forms of writing. Learn how to do that, and you'll learn how to write your play."

So, you're thumbing through a catalog, or you're in a bookstore, and you come across this colorful professional resource with a handsome poet on the front, and it's called *The Write Thing*, and you think, "Great, just what we need, another book on teaching writing!" But then you decide to pick it up. You take it home, open it up, read a little, and determine that it is at least interesting ... until, you get to this very scary word: POETRY. And you keep reading, and you quickly notice that it's ALL POETRY. The. Entire. Writing. Workshop. Is. Poetry.

Of course it's poetry, people! And it's the opposite of scary. It's soothing. It's the love poem your college sweetheart wrote to you. It's the rhyme you used to love to read and hear in elementary school. It's poetry because some of your favorite writers are poets: Maya Angelou, Shel Silverstein, Shakespeare. It's poetry because what teacher doesn't want their students' writing to be full of emotion. It's poetry because, as literary critic and educator Northrop Frye (2001) says, "If literature is to be properly taught, we have to start at its center, which is poetry, then work outwards to literary prose ... Poetry is the most direct and simple means of expressing oneself in words."

I've been teaching this writing workshop for more than 20 years and it's always been poetry because, the truth is, reading and writing poetry is fun and functional. Yes, I could have written a handbook for using fiction in a writing workshop, or memoir, or playwriting—wait, that's a good idea, stay tuned!— but for an introduction, there is no better literary vehicle to launch a writing workshop with than poetry.

As if I wasn't already thinking outside the box, I've added another uncommon component to the writing workshop: publishing. As a child of a book publisher and as a published author myself, you'll just have to trust me on this one, folks: The level of confidence your students will attain when they see their work available for public consumption is off the charts. It will be one of the highlights of their schooling. And your teaching as well.

I'd been an English teacher for more than 14 years, and I'd never seen anything like it. Poetry and Publishing. The workshop was so successful that we implemented it three years in a row. And when I moved to a new district, we did it again. I have witnessed students as young as 10 years of age walk taller because they were writers. Published writers. As administrators, it is our responsibility to provide opportunities for our students that are not only academic, but also empowering and transformational. That is education at its finest.

—Kim Hardwick, Principal,
Clayton Huey Elementary School, New York

When I wrote *The Crossover*, many publishers were afraid of it: "Kids, especially boys, don't like poetry," they told me, "and this book will never sell." I always believed that poetry, because it is so concise, rhythmic, and energetic, with tons of white space, would not only be unintimidating to students, but would be extremely appealing. I feel as strongly about *The Write Thing*. This writing workshop may be unconventional and uncommon, but it will work. It will have your students writing for their lives. And enjoying it. If you don't believe me, just ask seventh grader Ian, whom I met on a recent school visit:

> *I used to think poetry was boring. No fun, stupid, etc. After your book and presentation, I actually started to like it. It's interesting that you can use your own emotions and feelings to write something.*

Now, isn't that interesting?

"DON'T PLAY WHAT'S THERE, PLAY WHAT'S NOT THERE."
—MILES DAVIS

"WHEN YOU'RE TEACHING KIDS TO WRITE, YOU'RE TEACHING KIDS TO THINK.
WRITING IS THE WINDOW THROUGH WHICH ALL THINKING STARTS."
—SHERYL BLOCK

INTRODUCTION

Finding Your Writing Groove

Lucy Calkins says, "When students are published authors, they make reading-writing connections" (2001). In my 25 years of literacy work in schools around the world, I have witnessed this transformation firsthand, in particular with the Book-in-a-Day workshop that I founded in 2006. I took Calkins's innovative idea a step further and decided that the connection becomes exponentially stronger when the publishing component is, get this, student-run. How I arrived at this concept is a case study in child labor practice, happenstance, and improvisation.

I grew up with a father who wrote books and owned a publishing company. My mother wrote children's books and taught English. Books lined our walls and were stacked on floors in each room: biographies, history, fiction, textbooks, visual art, memoirs, children's literature, folklore, poetry. We read for fun, for punishment, for relaxation, even for competition. My very first writing workshop took place in our family room, where my siblings and I made up stories about the places we traveled and the people, real and imagined, we met, then shared them in family talent shows and as bedtime tales. This was our ritual. But, there was another side to this. I worked for my father's publishing company. And, I loathed it.

As an elementary and middle school student, I was involved from concept to shelf in the book publishing process. From typing to stapling direct-mail catalogues to exhibiting books at trade shows, I was immersed in literature and publishing daily while my friends played video games and rode bikes.

Don't get me wrong, I did get to play outside, but only after the inventory had been completed.

When I left for college, I had but one goal: to get as far away from books as fast as possible. So, I majored in biochemistry with every intention of becoming a doctor, until I encountered organic chemistry, and quickly changed my major to something more familial: English. After a series of classes and workshops with dynamic and inspiring creative writing professors such as Nikki Giovanni, my appreciation for story came full circle. I was back in my family room, only this time I decided that my literary pursuits would be life-sustaining, not just fodder for bedtime entertainment. I was going to write for a living. But not just pen to paper. My plans included hosting writing retreats, producing book festivals, publishing other writers, and teaching writing. So, I did. I was leading a full writerly life. And, I loved it.

Which brings us to Book-in-a-Day.

Creating a Student-Run Publishing Enterprise

From 1995–2005, I operated my own publishing company, continued conducting writing workshops in middle and high schools across the country, and wrote seven books, including *Do the Write Thing: 7 Steps to Publishing Success.* I'd been asked by novice writers, on a regular basis, how to publish a book. That book was my answer.

> Do the Write Thing *(DTWT) is like Publishing 101. It is designed for the novice who wants to learn the ABCs of book publishing. This reading will be similar to the first time you rode a bike. Remember when your father guided you down the sidewalk day after day? Then, one Saturday he let you ride by yourself. Just like that. And while you did fall a few times, eventually through practice, courage, and ingenuity, you mastered it. Unlike most publishing how-to books, which seem to get mired down in every possible detail and tedious direction, this book will give you a general map drawn in bright colors, and leave it up to you to chart your own course. I will impart my knowledge if you promise to tap into your creativity. My purpose is to teach you the mechanics of book publishing so that you feel confident enough to "ride by yourself."*
>
> —Preface of Do the Write Thing: 7 Steps to Publishing Success

The Beginning

I loved the bike riding metaphor in the preface. And, apparently so did a lot of other people. Suddenly, I became a budding expert in the field of self-publishing, and writers were turning to my text to help them find their literary stride. One such writer was Dana Davidson, a young adult novelist, who also happened to be an AP English teacher in Detroit, Michigan (a Newsweek/WDIV-TV Outstanding Teacher Awardee, in fact). She'd read my book and asked if I would consider facilitating a publishing workshop for her high school seniors. Over the course of the school year, her students had written fiction, essays, articles, axioms, and poems, and she wanted to reward them with a book. There was one hitch, however. She wanted me to teach the students so that they could do the actual publishing work themselves. That, and she only had one day for all of this to occur. Naturally, always one to embrace a challenge, I said "Yes!" and made my way to the Great Lake state.

KwameTime
Video for Teachers
The Write Thing
Overview
(See page 19.)

There were 35 students in each of Dana's five classes, which began at 7:30 in the morning and concluded at 4:30 in the afternoon. Like Bobby McFerrin leading a choir of singers in a musical experience that is completely improvisational, for those nine hours we created powerful melodies, rhythms, and textures. One class proofread, another created a title and designed a cover. Each group of students became a different department in our makeshift publishing company. By the end of the day, our performance, birthed out of a literal celebration of spontaneity, was complete. Two weeks later, copies of their paperback book, *Unspoken*, were delivered to the school, and a book party was held where students presented poems from the book to an excited audience of teachers, parents, friends, and educators. They autographed copies. They became proud authors. I bet you're wondering how it all went down, right? Keep reading ....

Transforming Young Lives

Word got around that I'd just helped a group of students publish a book in a day, and requests started coming in for me to work my magic at other schools. Unfortunately, the student work lacked the quality of the students in Dana's classes. The writing just didn't "behave." Rather than publish student work that was not up to par, I began offering a prerequisite writing workshop, with a focus on accessible and authentic poetry as the literary vehicle, prior to the publishing workshop. I began to model my unconventional writing workshop for teachers, sharing my tools to get students excited about writing. There had to be a structure, because it was called Book-in-a-Day, and I only had five hours with each group of students. Of course, I left enough room for flexibility within those five hours in case I had a creative epiphany or brainstorm (and I had many, thanks to the intellectual curiosity and diversity of the different students). Teachers were surprised that students, who typically had to be dragged to pen and paper, were now composing haiku.

Recently, while facilitating a middle school writing workshop in Singapore, a group of teachers shared with me their surprise that a boy who loathed reading and writing had become one of the stars of the writing workshop. He regularly volunteered correct answers to my questions; he eagerly shared his masterpieces with the group; and when students got a little loud and distracted, he shhhushed! them. Talk about the power of writing to transform young lives.

Solo Act: Deanna Nikaido
Book-in-a-Day Literacy Coach

When I was first introduced to the Book-in-a-Day literacy program, I was excited at the thought of helping a few students get their own work published, which was something no one else was doing. In many ways, in the beginning, it was beyond the students' (and teachers') dreams to actually do something significant like publish a book (in a day). There were so many unknowns. When working with young people, it's sometimes difficult to tell if or how you're making a difference. Thank goodness for the students who came up to us during break on the first day offering candid pages of their soul for us to read. But what about the students who had rarely, if ever, set foot upon the boat of their own words; never fully untied it from the dock, set it afloat, or let the throttle full out? I think what surprised me most were these students: the middle school boy who sat twirling his blank sheet of paper until the last hour of the day who ended up writing a love poem to his girl from the viewpoint of a football field; the third-grade boy who says he has nothing to write about and then stands up eager to share his poem about his brother who died and is surprised by his own tears; the high school girl who tells us how poetry saved her life; or the fifth grader from Canada who wrote, "Poems are like ships that take you away to places where you can let out what's inside of

Helping Students Find Their Voices

The goal of Book-in-a-Day was for students to "find their voices" so that they could uncover and express the woes and wonders of their world. And, it worked. Each workshop became a community of empowered voices. We laughed. We cried. We connected with literature in the same vital, electric, and life-giving ways I had as a child. After nine years and 76 schools, we created more than 5,000 engaged and excited student authors and publishers.

How to Use *The Write Thing*

The three-part writing workshop presented in this book—writing, publishing, and presenting—is my attempt to capture and share the tools, techniques, and energy of Book-in-a-

you. Poetry can be like wind, hard to catch but easy to feel. Those words that are jumbled inside of you can be expressed in a way to make a poem take you to a new world."

Since Book-in-a-Day's conception in 2006, we have worked with high schools, middle schools, elementary schools, the deaf community, and incarcerated youth, publishing over 3,000 student authors. Over the past 12 years, I have been amazed by the students' willingness to be candid. Some hoped that by being published, someone would read their words. Really listen. Maybe a parent or someone they liked or had a fight with. Some felt their poems could be megaphones traveling into the world to make a difference. Others just needed to share the best or worst moments of their day. Whatever the reason, these youths had a lot on their hearts and minds. They wanted to be heard.

For reasons I can't explain, poetry has always been a safe and acceptable way to say just about anything you want or need to express. It is the art of painting with words; building a bridge between the heart and mind; developing an emotional intelligence, which is even more necessary now in this Digital Age where connection is becoming more and more virtual. Poems look you in the eye.

I had no idea that this program to create a handful of student authors would catch fire in the way it has or become the compass these young people needed to be able to access their own unique voices; to say what they want to say as they journey into their own possibilities.

Day. Students participate in different types of writing: modeled, shared, interactive, and independent writing. *The Write Thing* and *Book-in-a-Day* are interchangeable terms. Think of this book as a guide to getting your students engaged with (and excited about) writing, reading, and speaking. It is designed for teachers who crave a literary jumpstart—part how-to, part inspiration.

The book is organized around a series of running features:

- Kwame QuickTips
- Solo Acts (voices from the field)
- Lessons in Action
- KwameTime videos
- You Can Too!
- Questions for Kwame
- And lots of poetry!

Lessons in Action are woven throughout the book at points of need. I've avoided designating grade levels because a good lesson is a good lesson—and I know you'll do what effective teachers always do: adapt it to fit the unique needs and interests of your students. You'll change it up if you work with older, sophisticated students, and you may simplify if your youngsters are just finding their way into the exciting new world of reading and writing. The Questions for Kwame throughout the book include both questions students ask when I visit them as well as frequently asked questions by teachers.

What about Time?

Out of necessity, our Book-in-a-Day workshop was one day, two at most. Your *The Write Thing* workshop doesn't have to follow such a rigid time line—it could be a week, a month, a semester—or better yet, a new way of life for you and your students. What's most important here is that you listen to the music of your students, be inspired, orchestrate, help them find their groove, and just jam!

Appendix and Digital Resources

Please look through the Appendixes of this book (pages 136–208) for a wealth of mini-lessons, guidelines, checklists, and forms to help you and your students during various stages of *The Write Thing* writing workshop. All student-facing activity pages mentioned throughout the book are provided in digital form for your easy reference and use. The poems shared throughout the book are also provided digitally to encourage you to display them for shared or modeled reading opportunities. See page 207 for more information about the digital resources provided with this product.

How to Access and Use KwameTime Videos

Interacting with students and teachers and sharing my love of poetry is such a big part of my job. And, I love it. Thing is, save for cloning, I can't be at every school. Unless …

Want to bring me into your classroom to assist with *The Write Thing*? Want a smiling, handsome poet to help jumpstart your writing workshop? This book includes a series of video clips of me in action. See page 207 for more information.

The clips are divided into two menus: 1) Kwame Guides Teachers and 2) Kwame Guides Students (and, as you'll notice, some clips work for both you and your students). The good news: you can watch them again and again, as many times as you might find useful—Kwame on an endless feedback loop (I may even slip a few poems in there for your enjoyment)!

KwameTime Videos

Part 1: Writing

"The writing workshop is a gathering place of passionate ideas and opinions. It is the room where our students can go to imagine and reimagine the world."

—Kwame Alexander

"POETRY IS
SERIOUS, PLAYFUL,
ALL-ENCOMPASSING, SPECIFIC,
DIVINE, INCOMPREHENSIBLE."
—WYNTON MARSALIS

CHAPTER ONE

Setting the Stage: Why Start with Poetry?

The world is hungry for words of hope, change, humor, and love, and writing workshop has the ability to conjure up the kind of meaningful and creative energy of the imagination that we all crave. Writing workshop is a gathering of passionate ideas and opinions. It is the birthplace of creative inspiration and illumination. It is the room where our students can go to imagine and reimagine the world for themselves, and for us. And, it must take place in 55 minutes, more or less.

Sure, classroom periods may dictate the amount of time we have for a writing workshop on a given day, but the most important thing is having designated writing time that students can expect, look forward to, and prepare for, mentally and otherwise. Still, because the amount of time is relatively short, some of our students may be a little harder to reach, either because of disinterest, fear, aptitude, or all three. No worries, I've got a foolproof method that guarantees you will reach even the most reluctant and recalcitrant of learners. It's worked for me in New York and Canada, summer writing programs and juvenile detention facilities, libraries and special needs programs, secondary and K–8 schools.

Want to create an immediate, vibrant, powerful writing workshop? Try poetry. Mounting evidence shows that writing is a crucial component of effective literacy instruction. When students are engaged regularly in writing, they show

KwameTime Video for Teachers
The Essential Importance of Writing
(See page 19.)

improvements in reading comprehension, math, science, and social studies (Reeves 2002). No one doubts the power of writing or the critical importance it should play in all students' lives:

> At its best, writing has helped transform the world. Revolutions have been started by it. Oppression has been toppled by it. And it has enlightened the human condition. American life has been richer because people like Rachel Carson, César Chavez, Thomas Jefferson, and Martin Luther King, Jr., have given voice to the aspirations of the nation and its people.
>
> —National Commission on Writing

With these findings in mind, getting children to be motivated, successful writers is a key component of effective literacy instruction, as well as overall student achievement, and there's no more accessible gateway than poetry. In my Book-in-a-Day workshops, I always began with poetry. Its inherent conciseness was less intimidating to even the most uneager writers, and it allowed students to produce a completed piece of work within the constraints of a five-hour workshop.

Poetry engages students in writing in ways that other genres do not. Because poetry does not have the same demands as prose, it offers students greater freedom (Routman 2001). The scope of poetry also allows students to express themselves in many different ways by experimenting with different styles and forms. Success with writing poetry can create enthusiasm that then makes other writing tasks feel more manageable.

QUESTIONS for KWAME

Can I do writing workshop with my English language learners?

Si! Vâng! Yes! Limited English does not mean limited creativity or limited feelings. Depending on the English level of a student, they may need to do some brainstorming ahead of time. Students can rely on picture cues and even translator apps and books to find the right words. You can also work one-on-one with a student to talk through their search for the perfect words. When their poem is finished, try to have two versions, one in English and the other in their first language. Over time, students can revise their poems and see how their growth in language skills affects their writing.

Solo Act: Ann Marie Stephens
Elementary School Teacher and Picture Book Author

Kwame poses the question "Why poetry?" My first graders pose very different questions, such as "What is poetry? Is it something we can eat? Can I have some?" I love the idea of using a "creative jumpstart" to begin a workshop. Kwame reminds us that there is emotion attached to poetry. I choose to jumpstart through the use of Leo Lionni's book, Frederick. *All the mice in the book are working hard to gather essentials for the upcoming winter. Frederick appears to be doing nothing, but in reality, he is gathering words—beautiful, dreamy, rich words. These same words come out during the harsh winter as warm, spirit-lifting poetry for his mouse friends and him. After reading, we reflect on Frederick's words, his poem, and their impact on the other mice. We talk about feelings and then we use a large piece of paper to make a class list under the heading "Poetry Feels..." If the class struggles to name the emotions, we look back on the illustrations in the book. After we think the list is complete, I read a funny poem (often one by Shel Silverstein). The kids giggle and make comments, and suddenly we have more emotions to add to our list. We always save the list for later when we do list poems.*

Kwame QuickTip

You can fill *The Write Thing* writing workshop with a range of writing across genres—which establishes the purposes for which we write: narrative, informative/explanatory, and opinion/argument. For easy-to-launch, guaranteed success, it's hard to beat poetry.

I have a guiding belief in the power of poetry to connect with young writers, reluctant and avid, in transformative and profound ways. Georgia Heard (1998) suggests that we use poems as transitions, immersing students in accessible poems first and then building on that foundation. I couldn't agree more. Poetry is the bridge to get our children to appreciate and understand how to imagine and reimagine possibility through creative language, to embrace more complex and longer forms of literature.

The Essential Joy of Poetry

Poetry is a powerful method to engage students in writing that is meaningful to them; yet, poetry is not given as much attention as it deserves. It is a genre that is neglected throughout upper elementary, middle, and high school, as well as in teacher education courses (Certo, Apol, Wibbens, & Yoon 2010). There are many reasons (and excuses) why more poetry is not in classrooms. Louann Reid says teachers "believe they have not been prepared to teach poetry. Lack of experience, lack of preparation, and lack of confidence quickly add up to lack of interest if not complete apathy" (2006, 9). The disappearance of poetry from classrooms has thus generated a cycle of indifference among students (Parr and Campbell 2006).

Solo Act: Marjory Wentworth
Poet Laureate of South Carolina

I started the day by having the children write wish poems. Each poem began with the line "I wish." This writing exercise comes from the book Wishes, Lies, and Dreams: Teaching Children to Write Poetry *by Kenneth Koch. Mr. Koch taught poetry in New York City elementary schools, and this book is the result of those experiences. Now, just imagine what happens when you ask school children, or anyone else for that matter, what they wish for? In order to demystify the poetry-writing process, I had the children begin by writing a class poem about things they wished for. Each child contributed a line, and when I put them all together we had a poem. It was easy, quick, and FUN.*

When students are enjoying themselves, they pay closer attention, they follow directions, and they care about what they're writing because it matters a lot to them. The stillness and concentration that happens whenever students begin writing poems is extraordinary to witness.

These third graders at Dunston Elementary School in North Charleston, South Carolina, wished for all sorts of fascinating things—new bicycles, a four-wheeler, a baby sister, a baby brother, more bling, a pinkie ring, a pair of kittens, a Jacuzzi, a swimming pool, a laptop, a black-and-white dog, a kazillion dollars, and so on. One little boy wrote that he

This changes today, people.

In her text, *In the Middle*, Nancie Atwell observes, "Seventy years ago, fully half the literature taught to fourth graders in the United States was poetry. Today it's 97 percent prose and just 3 percent poetry" (1998, 416). Don't get me wrong, I love that my nine-year-old daughter is reading *Charlotte's Web* and *Ramona the Brave*, but I'd also love it if she were learning Gwendolyn Brooks's "We Real Cool" (now, that'd be real cool!). Thing is, we're kind of afraid of poetry. For so long, we've been taught that poetry is staid, complicated, unfamiliar, and now many of us believe it. How did this happen? When did poetry become something intimidating and inaccessible? It often happens, unfortunately, in a middle and high school English classroom, but parents and teachers can turn this around.

wished for a friend. A number of children wished for things for their teachers—a big yellow diamond, a pink Cadillac. No one suggested they do this; the generosity came naturally.

The most amazing part of the day came when I was about to leave. A little boy named Jonathan stood right in front of me and started talking about his brain. Our conversation went something like this:

"Do you know how your brain has two parts to it? The top part that you use most of the time and that deep part that you hardly ever use?"

I nodded, wondering where this was going.

"Well," he continued, looking up at me with enormous sincerity, "When I was writing my poem, I used that deep part of my brain the whole time."

"Don't you use that deep part a lot in school?"

"Not really," he said, shaking his head.

"That's creativity you're describing. It's a great feeling."

"Creativity," he repeated. "That's what you call my really deep brain working?"

"Exactly."

We must remember that many of the essential joys of poetry are the first ones we experience with language. Young children delight in the sounds they make and hear. The first words that children speak emerge like a repetitive chant. In that way, a child's first words are like a first poem. Children love to rhyme, and many children's first books are rhymed books. Rhyming is fun. Words are fun. Let's also remember that young children already experience the world the way a poet does. Have you ever taken a toddler by the hand and tried to walk a few blocks? They notice everything—the sound of every passing car or insect, a coin shining on the sidewalk. Children's senses inform them as they move through the world. This is exactly how poets experience the world, too; which is why, when you read a poem, you can picture the images described or repeat a line over and over in your head, just to hear the sheer beauty of the sounds that the words make. These words, when strung together in a particular way, bring you joy. In some ways, it is that simple. Poetry must be enjoyed at this primal level.

My goal in this book is to help everyone find that joy again. To help spark a whole new relationship with poetry. I'm not saying that this book is going to change your teaching life, but I do know that since the age of 12 when I wrote my very first poem for Mother's Day, poetry has changed mine. I've spent a lifetime writing poetry that matters, and now I want to teach you and your students to do the same.

The Transformative Power of Poetry

A poem is a small but powerful thing. One third grader put it this way: Poetry is an egg with a horse inside it. It has the power to reach inside you, to ignite something in you, and to change you in ways you never imagined. There is a feeling of connection and communion—with the author and with the subject—when we read a poem that articulates our deepest feelings. That connection can be a vehicle on the road to creativity and imagination. Poems are the human

QUESTIONS for KWAME

Out of every type of writing, why did you choose poetry?
I didn't; it chose me. I read so much of it as a kid, it just seeped into my head and my heart and it consumed me. Also, because I love saying a whole lot in very few words. The white space is pretty spectacular. I love the words that aren't there that the reader fills in. How cool is that?

soul condensed for our pleasure. When done right, they can inspire us—in our classrooms and in our homes—to write our own journeys, to find our own voices.

During one of my very first author visits, I remember a high school English teacher warning me that her students would not be engaged or responsive to my presentation, as many of them abhorred poetry. I asked her if she taught poetry, and she shared that she had taught it begrudgingly, as it was not her favorite either. I could relate.

When I was in high school, I was not interested in the poetry we learned in AP English. It was inaccessible, unrelatable and, quite frankly, boring. That is not to say that it was not valuable, because it was; these were the literary stalwarts of the canon, after all. True, we were learning, but our human souls weren't being moved in some significant way. And if you want a student to be moved by poetry, if you want to be moved by poetry, then you must share poetry with which you (and they) connect on an emotional level.

There's something that happened with poetry along the way where people started thinking of a measurable substance—you get it or you don't get it. Just sweep that out of the room, and create a sense of love. What you don't need for the teaching of poetry, I think, is to feel as if you're an expert ... but you do have to find places of real love within yourself, for lines, for voices, for topics, for ways of writing, for styles that will help you create a mood, an atmosphere where poetry becomes contagious.
—Naomi Shihab Nye

AND I HAVE YOU

Rain has drops
Sun has shine
Moon has beams
That make you mine

Rivers have banks
Sands for shores
Hearts have heartbeats
That make me yours

Needles have eyes
Though pins may prick
Elmer has glue
To make things stick

Winter has Spring
Stockings feet
Pepper has mint
To make it sweet

Teachers have lessons
Soup du jour
Lawyers sue bad folks
Doctors cure

All and all
This much is true
You have me
And I have you

—*Nikki Giovanni*

So many of us have been immersed, since grade school, in staid and incomprehensible poetry, that we feel disconnected from it. We've been taught that to understand a poem, we must first dissect it (we dissect frogs, not poetry), and so we've forgotten what poetry feels like. We've forgotten that sense of joy that comes from reading between the lines. We must

seek out and find poetry that helps us rediscover that sense of love that Naomi Shihab Nye speaks of. (I've included some mentor texts on page 61 for your perusal.) Let's use poetry as a ladder in the writing workshop, carefully and intentionally taking each step and working our way up. This way, we are more apt to climb our way to a more heightened appreciation of language and literature.

There are a plethora of good reasons for teaching poetry in schools. Faced with the demands of data-driven decision-making and a cacophony of instructional practices, teachers have to discern the approaches that will have the greatest impact on student engagement and learning, as well as on growth (Holbrook 2005). Poetry instruction offers a range of possibilities for improving reading and writing and increasing student motivation (Cecil 1994; Routman 2001).

When you hear the word *poetry* you might think, "That's not part of my curriculum," or "I don't have time." The first may be true but the second doesn't have to be. Poetry is a form of writing, a way of expressing oneself that can be incorporated into your time and curricular constraints. There is no rule that says that poetic expression cannot contain details of the Civil War, an interpretation of a piece of fiction, or even the process behind mathematical computations. If your students have an understanding of what you are teaching, why not let them respond in any form—including poetry? An I Remember poem (page 150) can be just that—What do you want your students to remember about animal habitats? Challenge them to write an I Am Pizzazz poem (page 148) from the perspective of a person in history. There are endless opportunities to incorporate poetry into your required content. Once given the choice, many students will ask to write in poetry form instead of more traditional ways. Let them have the freedom to explore. And watch their growth in literacy explode.

What's more, poetry addresses the demands of higher standards and more. Need to help your students craft precise words, phrases, and telling details? Try poetry. Nudging your students to wrap their writing heads around compare and contrast? Poetry is your best friend. What about domain-specific vocabulary and figurative meaning? You simply can't beat poetry for pure "turbocharged" skill work—when that's where you need to go with your students. As poet Paul Janeczko (2011) writes:

> As teachers today, everything we teach has to be turbocharged with skills and the promise of advancing our students academically … And here's the cool thing: poetry can get you there. It is inherently turbocharged. Poets distill a novel's worth of content and emotion in a handful of lines. The literary devices you need to teach are all there ….

So, let's try to change the conversation, create a different feeling, forge a new relationship with poetry. Ever listen to Wynton Marsalis and his Big Band live? Yeah, me neither, but go online and watch it. Instinctively, intimately, and immediately, you feel smarter, more connected. To yourself. Poetry does the same thing. It has the power to reach students, tap into their emotional intelligence while allowing them to freely and openly express themselves. It can be the school where our children go to learn to write well. And here's the thing, they are already writing poetry, in their journals, notebooks, on walls, online, in their minds. They are ready to play, and writing workshop sets the stage for them.

PICTURING YOU

I am not a painter
Browns and blues
We get along
But we
are not close
I am no
Van Gogh
But give me
Plain paper
A dull pencil
Some scotch
And I will
Hijack your curves
Take your soul
Hostage
Paint a portrait
So colorful and delicate
You just may have to
Cut off my ear

—Kwame Alexander

Vision and Validation

Once, I met a young woman at a book signing. She looked smart, dressed classy, and smiled a lot. And, to top it off, she'd purchased my book. She came up to the table for an autograph, and I was spellbound. Words failed me. (Kinda ironic, right?) I lacked the confidence to let her know just how I felt in that moment: I was crushing. We exchanged email addresses, and I did what any self-respecting poet would do. (See poem on page 31.)

After she read the poem I'd written her, she sent me an email that said, "Here's my number, give me a ring." And a few years later, get this, she married me.

Kathy Perfect claims poetry "nurtures a love and appreciation for the sound and power of language. Poetry can help us see differently, understand ourselves and others, and validate our human experience. It ... enhances thinking skills and promotes personal connections ..." (1999, 728). Poetry sure worked for me, and it can definitely work for you and your students.

POET and POETRY Acronyms

Teachers can share these acronyms, giving solid examples for each letter. The acronyms help poets to steer clear of crafting clichés.

Present creative ideas
Original content is a must
Exercise abstract muscles
Train your senses

Powerful words: Enchilada, Cicada
Other ideas: Things that others may not consider
Exploring ideas: Write about your interests
Trying different styles: Experiment with form
Relying on instincts: Write about what matters to you
Your work is meaningful: Enjoy expressing yourself

—*Created by Kwame Alexander and Van G. Garrett*

Solo Act: Marcelle Haddix
Dean's Associate Professor in Reading and Language Arts Syracuse University

In my work in community writing projects with black adolescent youth, I am often struck by the responses I get from young people when I ask the question, "Are you a writer?" More often than not, they answer "no" because they make an immediate connection between writing and school-sanctioned literacy practices. That question, however, assumes negative responsibilities. That is, based on the way I frame the question, young people are left to answer either "yes" or "no." Because of the limited responses my question yields, I encourage more dialogue about multiple ways of writing and expression and writing for multiple purposes and contexts. With further exploration, young people identify as writers in self-sanctioned literacy practices, such as writing online via networking sites such as Instagram or Twitter and/or writing poetry and lyrics. Writing for school is defined by timed writing tasks for standardized exams or the demonstration of the conventions of writing, and many of the young people I work with feel inept in such tasks. In order for young people to take on identities as writers, they have to be apprenticed into writing communities.

YOU CAN TOO!

1. How have you taught poetry in the past? What were the positive effects of using poetry with your students?

2. In what ways might using poetry change your students' feelings about writing workshop in your classroom?

3. Make a list of poems that have affected you throughout your life. Which powerful poems from your life could be used to introduce poetry to your students? Add to this list throughout the year.

"WE NEED TO ANTICIPATE HOW WE WILL INITIATE, SCAFFOLD, AND GUIDE THE CLASSROOM COMMUNITY TOWARD AN EVER-DEEPENING INVOLVEMENT."
—LUCY CALKINS

CHAPTER TWO

Launching the Writing Workshop

I love jazz (you've certainly figured that out by now), but I am also a huge '80s soft rock fan. Journey, Tina Turner, Wham! (I probably shouldn't be admitting that here), Phil Collins, and, of course, The Police, are gods to me. I remember going to Sting's Soul Cages tour and, like all the other 50,000 fans, hoping the opening act would perform a quick set so we could go on with the real show. And, when we saw the opening act—a tall guy with red and blue dreadlocks and an African drum hanging from around his neck—we prayed that It. Would. Be. Over. Soon. Then Vinx opened his mouth, and a booming melodic bass came out. And when his palms hit the djembe, it spoke to us. And it was jazz. And pop. And rock. And lots of SOUL, all wrapped into one stellar opening 30-minute performance that had us all enthralled and wishing it would never end.

Begin with a Thrill

When my daughter has playdates at our house, I'm often in charge of activities. Before the pool or the swings, I facilitate a haiku scavenger hunt. The girls must search for little stickies with emotions and objects written on them (e.g., anger, bananas) and then draft haiku. There are prizes for the winners. The thrill of adventure throughout my house is bananas. (See what I did there?) I posit that the writing workshop must begin with the same thrill. An opening activity that corrals the soul, gets students primed and ready for the major exploration of wonder and woe that awaits. Since this is a writing workshop, it is imperative that the opening act introduce students to a beginning writing activity, to get the juices flowing.

Creative Jumpstarts

Over the years, I've employed a range of creative jumpstarts to get students ready and eager to write, many of which I've borrowed from my own teachers.

Discussion

When I took Nikki Giovanni's advanced poetry workshop at Virginia Tech, each class began with a discussion that sometimes quickly turned into a heated debate (and occasionally, when we discussed political issues, an argument). And then she simply said, "Now write." And we did. We were eager to share our thoughts and ideas on paper and express why we were so passionate about our views. It was as if we needed that jumpstart to prepare ourselves for the real work, for the literary journey that she wanted us to take, the journey that we didn't even know we were on.

Allowing students to lead the discussion ensures that the topic will be of interest to them. Sometimes they want to talk about their dreams the night before, the stress of school, the latest pop star controversy, or even a community tragedy. I've found that having an open, honest dialogue with students fosters a sense of community in the classroom, which is the kind of environment a productive writing workshop craves.

Music

In one of our Book-in-a-Day workshops, I had a coach bring out her guitar and play a song. Some of the students laughed at the randomness of live music in a writing workshop, but all listened, and when it was over they applauded. Immediately following the performance, I asked each student to free-write a paragraph on the song they'd just listened to—about how

Kwame QuickTip

There are hundreds of poets in your city (check your local writing center, cafe open mic, or independent bookstore for recommendations) who would love the opportunity to come to your class and read/perform. Poets from faraway places might even Skype with you. Of course, you can also read your own verse or recite a favorite poem.

they felt, about what it meant, about the title, anything about the song they felt compelled to write. No rules, just write. Some students needed a further prompt, and so I gave them the first line of their free-write: *This is what I know.* Now, every classroom doesn't have an accomplished musician who can whip out an instrument and belt out a polished number, but we all have access to music. Begin each writing workshop by letting students listen to music (especially jazz). Not only does the music empower critical and creative thinking, high-speed intellectual engagement with the ideas of others, self-actualization, and confidence, but if you choose the right song, it creates feelings of well-being and sometimes, euphoria.

Storytelling

Finally, doing a fun, interactive read aloud for your younger students or sharing a personal story for your older ones, are great ways to break the ice, to get students' attention, to begin the workshop in an enriching manner.

It's Mother's Day, 1982, and I have a total of $2.67 in my piggy bank. My choices for gifts are sorrowfully limited. I venture to the local drug store to peruse the aisles and notice a "gold" picture frame on sale for $1.99. Instantly I know that if I make this purchase I will have enough change for a pack of bubble gum. This becomes the defining moment in my gift shopping. It is only after I leave the store, skipping along and popping bubbles, do I figure out what will go inside the frame: A picture. Of me! Unfortunately, none of the photographs fit inside of the frame, and I can't find a pair of scissors in the house. And then it hits me. My mother is a storyteller. She loves making words dance across our imaginations, swirling and dipping, soaring and diving. And my sisters and I laugh and cry and oooh and ahhh when she spins a tale. My mother is a lover of words. So, if I can't give her a picture of me, I will do the next best thing.

I sit down at the typewriter and type out a poetic masterpiece with a very original title: "Mother's Day." After reading the poem (it takes her a while to finish it, not because it is too complex, but because she keeps having to flick "gold" specks off of her hand), a succession of teardrops scuttle down her face. We hug and she lets me watch television until I fall asleep (as a rule, we weren't allowed to watch television in our home, except on Fridays for one hour, so this was a big deal). I dream that night about other ideas for poems and stories to share with my family and friends. I figure if my words get this type of encouraging emotional response, maybe I should write a poem a day. After all, it only took me a half an hour to write the Mother's Day ode. This is the day I fall in love with poetry.

Thirty years and 25 published books later, and I'm still in love. The incandescent reaction I received from my mother on that day in 1982 remains with me today. It's the main reason I continue to write poetry. Poetry is supposed to take you somewhere, make you feel ... something. I remember liking that feeling. Now, the poem I wrote back then was horrendous, and thus I won't share it here in these pages, on grounds that it might incriminate me in the world poetry court. However, here's a haiku I wrote for her, much later in life:

there would be no books
without the childhood tales
the playful way you loved

Invariably, the shared or independent writing that comes out of these creative jumpstarts is some combination of humorous, heart-wrenching, and revelatory. The writing isn't judged for craft, and sharing is encouraged. We want the students enthralled in the creative process. We want them excited, not bored. We want them to embrace the writing, not be intimidated by it. How we open our workshop will set the stage for how our students act and react.

All these strategies have worked for me, but none have worked better than just diving right in between the lines of a good poem.

Pull a Poem Out of Your Pocket

Teaching poetry is often a balancing act between the technical aspects of form and the creative aspects of writing. Reciting rules and stressing form can stifle creativity or turn students (and teachers) off of poetry. That's why Broadway is so important. (Yes. I just said Broadway!) Start your workshop with an activity that lets the words leap off the page and onto the STAGE. Make the words come alive. The best way for you and your students to see that poetry is fun and cool, is to see it. To listen to it. Live!

The aim of this chapter is to introduce (or reintroduce) you and your students to the beauty and magic of other people's poetry. To proclaim what poetry is (fun and cool) and deny what it is not (boring). To demystify one of the world's most ancient forms of literary language. To help you feel comfortable in an environment of rhythm, rhyme, concise wordplay, and emotion, powered by poetry. Don't worry, you won't have to write any original poetry in this chapter. Promise! This is strictly about taking a dip in the pool, or to continue the jazz metaphor, to sample some different tunes, get a feel for what we like, and perhaps, for what we didn't know we liked.

After college, I moved to Arlington, Virginia, to embark upon my literary journey. To become a poet. I was advised by countless friends and family, that "poetry doesn't sell, so get a real job." They didn't think it was a worthy career choice. They didn't understand poetry. In some ways, they were afraid of it, because most of the verse they'd been exposed to during their schooling was staid and hieroglyphic, at best. Boring, at worst. Does that sound familiar? I've met countless teachers over the years who've expressed this same sentiment. This was my first clue, that if you want people to be interested in poetry, you simply must expose them to interesting poetry. Makes sense, right? Same applies for us educators.

On the bus to my real job each day, as I prepared to toil away in Corporate America, I read poetry. Interesting poetry. I laughed at the rhymes of Langston Hughes and smiled at the passion of Pablo Neruda. The words came alive for me, and this daily immersion served as tremendous inspiration for my own writing. It got me revved up, excited, ready to tell my own stories. And that I did, during lunch. Sneakily at my desk. I even wrote a few haiku on breaks with the smokers even though I didn't smoke.

This is where I believe we must begin our poetry or writing workshops with our students. Pull a poem out of your pocket. An accessible poem. A relatable poem. A poem that you like. Even better, a poem that you love.

THE SUMMARY

We were as tight as
a closed book
until someone opened us
and read the pages
read our secrets.

Then you wrote a summary
of the book
and read it aloud in class.
The rumors are spreading.

What kind of friend are you?

—*Mariam, Grade 6*

QUESTIONS for KWAME

Where do you get inspiration from?
From my daughters, from reading, from artwork, from life. I am a willing participant in life. I walk through life paying attention to everything, eavesdropping on everyone, and I find myself inspired by the littlest things—a smile on a rainy day—and the biggest—Love.

Solo Act: Ann Marie Stephens
Elementary School Teacher and Picture Book Author

On Monday, I asked my first graders, "Is there a poem in your pocket?" Everyone checked their pockets and answered with a chorus of "No's." I then read "Hug O' War" by Shel Silverstein. (A poem that's relatable and rhymes is essential for this first round.) We took a little time to discuss the poem and what it meant to each of them, and we kept individual copies to practice with throughout the week. Practice can mean reading to a classmate, a stuffed animal, the teacher, or reading in the mirror. On Thursday, I gave a big reminder to "wear pockets" to school on Friday. On Friday morning, my students practically knocked me down to show how many pockets they had. Everyone tucked a small copy of the poem into a pocket. The kids took turns standing up in front of the class (either solo or in small groups) and they performed the poem—some very shyly. Some knew the words, some memorized them, but THEY ALL READ! Their classmates applauded and they asked to go again. We tucked the poems back in our pockets and took them home to share with families.

As a follow up to "Poem in Your Pocket," you can make a large paper pocket out of poster board. Hang it on a bulletin board or wall. Call it your "Poetry Pocket" or "Pocketful of Poetry." (#pocketfulofpoetry) Each week, slip in a copy of the poems you've used from any of your workshop activities. The pocket will be stuffed! At the end of the year, randomly pull out poems and have a poetry jam. If you have leftover copies of each poem, make an additional pocket to hang outside your room on your door or wall. Encourage anyone in the school to reach in and take poems to read and to put in their own pockets.

QUESTIONS for KWAME

When do I introduce poetry?

You can introduce poetry whenever you want. It's possible to start the first week of school or halfway through the year. You can do a little each day or once a month. Your class can take the fast track to publication or use the entire year to build on your collection. Poetry does not need to be a separate unit of study. It can be incorporated into any subject.

Start. Class. With. A. Poem.

Read it, recite it, play it, show it, or let your students perform it.

- Perhaps it might be Shel Silverstein's "Ickle Me Tickle Me Pickle Me Too," or let students listen to Queen Latifah reciting a poem from Nikki Giovanni's *Hip Hop Speaks to Children: A Celebration of Poetry With a Beat.*

- Maybe you show students an online clip of a young poet performing on HBO's *Brave New Voices.*

- If you're really good, you might pull out a poem you wrote in high school, or one you shared at the open mic no one knows you attended. If students see you taking a risk, being vulnerable, they will be more willing to do the same.

Whatever your choice, it's important to begin your class or workshop by sharing a poem that will resonate with your audience. See my list of recommended poems on the next page.

The Students Are the Curriculum

One day, six months into my first "real job," while toiling away on a spreadsheet, I received a call that would change my life. The call came on my home answering machine, which I checked every half-hour—for the full-time poetry job that I knew was coming. As it turned out, the coordinator of the local "poet-in-the-schools" program wanted to know if I could

Kwame QuickTip

During your writing lessons/workshop, keep a notebook or box or jar of poems handy (or ask one or two students to do so). Always have a poem ready that can illustrate teachable moments. Know your audience—present poems that are relevant. Feel free to use your own poems or poems that you feel will connect and resonate with students. Poems are also perfect for those times when you feel like your students are losing interest (or heaven forbid, you are losing interest).

Recommended Poems

Grades K–2

- "Snowball" by Shel Silverstein
- "Now We Are Six" by A. A. Milne
- "Snail" by Langston Hughes
- "Kitty Caught a Caterpillar" by Jack Prelutsky
- "The Swing" by Robert Louis Stevenson
- "Clouds" by Christina Rossetti

Grades 3–5

- "Colors" by Shel Silverstein
- "Puzzlement" by Gwendolyn Brooks
- "'Hope' Is the Thing with Feathers" by Emily Dickinson
- "Jabberwocky" by Lewis Carroll
- "Butter" by Elizabeth Alexander
- "Knoxville, Tennessee" by Nikki Giovanni
- "My Shadow" by Robert Louis Stevenson

Secondary

- "Once the Dream Begins" by Yusef Komunyakaa
- "I, Too" by Langston Hughes
- "Ode to a Large Tuna in the Market" by Pablo Neruda
- "Do Not Go Gentle Into That Good Night" by Dylan Thomas
- "Annabel Lee" by Edgar Allan Poe
- "Oranges" by Gary Soto

visit a high school to lead a writing workshop for a group of urban, "alternative" high school students. This seemed easy enough, I thought, preparing my mini-lesson on plot and characters, metaphor and simile, e. e. cummings and Alice Walker. I was ready to help these students do the write thing. I stood and screamed so loud, my cubicle-mates thought I'd won the lottery. I accepted her offer, and gladly thanked her for the $25 honorarium she'd indicated was customary, though I probably shouldn't have turned in my resignation letter.

As I approached this first school visit, and the security guard walked me to the class, I heard all kinds of hoots and hollers, music and mayhem. Who were these rambunctious, bombastic hooligans, I wondered. I walked into the class I'd been assigned, and realized that the hooligans were, in fact, my audience for the next hour. As I scanned my audience, it dawned on me that "alternative" was code for "students who were kicked out of regular school for reasons ranging from too violent to too pregnant to too difficult to teach anything to, let alone poetry."

From the second I was introduced to the class by the teacher who seemed even less interested than her students, I knew that my entire outline, strategy, plan was moot. How would I be able to teach them about denouement and rising action and figurative language if they were sleeping, dancing, arguing? And they were. In that moment, I realized that my little curriculum, which I called the *Practice of Encouraging Thought* (P.O.E.T.) needed to be revamped, revised, reimagined. Immediately, on the spot. In less than 90 seconds, I realized that the curriculum was the students. I didn't articulate it like this, then, but I knew I had less than a few minutes to grab their attention, to make a connection, if there was going to be any writing taking place, and there was only one way to do that. I would need to risk embarrassment, take a creative leap, dance naked on the floor. And, so I stood on a chair

QUESTIONS for KWAME

What do I do with the student who doesn't feel inspired or poetic?

Help them find inspiration. Survey them for their likes and dislikes. (We can be passionate about both.) Give them the freedom to explore or research their ideas, and then assist them in a brainstorming session. Do they love video games? Do they dislike strange foods? Any subject can become the topic for a poem. If your student lacks confidence, start with an easy poem style that is suitable for the grade level you teach.

and hollered a poem I'd discovered in an anthology in my parents' garage. It's called "One Thousand Nine-Hundred & Sixty-Eight Winters ..." by Jackie Earley. Go ahead; look it up.

At first there was silence, and then one of the sleeping kids lifted his head. Another student took off her headphones. The teacher even stopped reading her newspaper. All laughed. One moment I was Ella Fitzgerald singing "Satin Doll" live in Hollywood, 1969, when, in the middle of the song, her microphone malfunctioned (true story). And in the next moment, like Ella, I was scatting and riffing my way through the performance in front of a captivated audience.

One benefit to choosing a poem that was so vivid, so full of metaphor and message, is that it connected emotionally with the students, it made them think, and that provoked discussion—ranging from weather to racism to isolation. Discussing the merits and meaning of a poem is yet another way to get students intimately invested in the writing process, and inevitably, writing workshop. One student in the class was so moved by the poem that she asked me for my copy of it, rewrote it in her notebook, and claimed "this poem gets me."

I recited a few more poems in the workshop, and within 15 minutes, I had the attention of most every student, and the writing workshop commenced.

A ton of laughter filled the classroom that was now visited by neighboring students and teachers. Even the principal visited. By poem number five, a rhymed love quatrain I'd written for my then-girlfriend-now-wife (see poem on page 45), the "hooligans" were not only attentive, they were completing the end-rhymes of each stanza. Teachers from other classes

Kwame QuickTip

Play some instrumental jazz while your students are writing. Research shows that people who listen to jazz are more creative and way cooler. Seriously, Valorie Salimpoor, a neuroscientist at the Rotman Research Institute says that "when you hear music that you find intensely pleasurable, it triggers a dopamine response." Okay, so maybe don't play too much, lest you end up with a ton of awkward love poems!

Kwame QuickTip

Kylene Beers, a past president of National Council of Teachers of English, wrote an entire book about helping kids who struggle. She writes, "First, teachers want to help the struggling [learners] who sit in their classrooms; second, those students want to be helped; and, third, the right instruction can make a difference" (2003, 1). Throughout the many years I've been working with kids, I've found there's no better pathway to success, for even the most disengaged kids, than poetry—reading what other poets have written and especially having a chance to write their own.

were stopping by to see what all the quiet was about. I'd recited poetry that connected with these young people, and they were eating it up. For the next 50 minutes, I talked about Pablo Neruda and Langston Hughes (some of the students even knew "A Dream Deferred"); we debated whether rap was poetry; I discussed the power of expressing feelings and thought through free verse and haiku. One student even recited "The Raven" by Edgar Allan Poe. And then, they wrote.

I wish I still had some of the writings the students created that day. They weren't masterpieces by any stretch of the imagination, but they were stepping stones. They were ladders to more writing. To greater writing. They were confidence boosters for each of us. They were cool glasses of fresh limeade on a steamy summer day. And, it is that kind of comfort and heart that must be summoned at the beginning of any writing workshop.

CONVERSATION AFTER LUNCH

"it's not that i don't
love you," she says. "indeed,
i want to kiss you...

"to lasso your lips
tame them, ride them, rein them in
to my stable, but

"first, my love, you must agree
to commit ... to a breath mint"

—*Kwame Alexander*

The Importance of Free Writing

Each of the beginning activities mentioned previously always concluded with an independent writing exercise, often journaling or free writing, which is both a source of inspiration and a stepping stone to self-enlightenment. When we free write, we just let our words out, all of them. And while some of what we write may just be the sludge necessary to clear out before the treasure unfolds, we also may go back and read what we wrote and find a shining nugget that we can use for later writing. (*The best way to have a good idea, is to have lots of ideas.*)

Lesson in Action

Prompting Free Writing

Allow students to write about whatever they want—for 10–20 minutes, just enough to get their fingers dancing on the page. It can be a journal entry, it can be a poem, it can be a response to something they heard or read during the activity. Some students will not know what to write about, so have some prompts ready:

- Write a letter to your dog or cat.

- Write a letter to the "you" last year.

- Write a six-word memoir about your summer.

- Write about your favorite movie. Do not tell me about that movie, just write about how it made you feel.

- Write about a terrible dream you've had.

Some students will want to share their work at the end of this exercise, which should always be encouraged and praised, not necessarily for the content, but for the effort. In addition to building excitement, we are also trying to build confidence.

The Magic Between the Lines

The first step to helping your students appreciate the sweetness of this ancient language of love is to give them a sampling. Let them taste the magic between the lines. Feed them some of the beauty and pain and happiness and tragedy and hopefulness that is poetry. What's in your pocket?

HOW TO EAT A POEM

Don't be polite.
Bite in.
Pick it up with your fingers and lick the juice that
     may run down your chin.
It is ready and ripe now, whenever you are.

You do not need a knife or fork or spoon
or plate or napkin or tablecloth.

For there is no core
or stem
or rind
or pit
or seed
or skin
to throw away.

—*Eve Merriam*

YOU CAN TOO!

1. How can poetry create stepping stones to more writing in your classroom?

2. In what ways do you make sure your curriculum is "the students"?

3. What poem do you plan to have in your pocket for your next writing workshop?

"MY JOB IS TO NOT ONLY INSTRUCT POETS ON HOW TO SEE, BUT ALSO TO TEACH THEM HOW TO LOOK FOR THINGS OTHERS OVERLOOK, OMIT, AND/OR OSTRACIZE."
—VAN G. GARRETT, POET AND MIDDLE SCHOOL ENGLISH TEACHER

CHAPTER THREE

Preparing to Write

Teaching poetry is an opportunity to foster the ways that poets see, think, and write. The art of being observant serves poets well. Our goal is to teach poets how to think and then give them the tools to find, refine, and redefine their voices, in order to share their thoughts.

Many successful writers approach their craft in metacognitive ways. Writers should be aware of their instincts. However, they should not be afraid to dance naked on the floor, to take risks.

Now that your students are amped up, hopefully excited about the workshop, it's time to give them the tools to properly channel this enthusiasm and confidence.

Emotions, Meaning, and More

In a workshop in upstate New York, I asked a sixth grader to define poetry. He responded that poetry was "a get together of emotions." How wonderful is that? Can't you just imagine words and feelings partying together? (Of course, there's no DJ at this party, it must be a live jazz band!) I then asked if he thought poems could be bad, and he, like most of his classmates, emphatically answered, "No, because it's just your feelings, and your feelings can't be bad or wrong."

**KwameTime
Video for Students
*Defining Poetry***
(See page 19.)

Nikki Giovanni likes to say that there are some poems that don't behave, that are uninteresting, and it's important for our students to know and learn how to avoid *misbehaving*.

Imagine coming over to my house for brownies, and they're salty, unsweet, and so hard they could chip a tooth. Would you consider the brownies to be good? Well, like brownies, poetry must have the right ingredients, be prepared properly, and sweetened just right. Otherwise, it's not very good. I use the baking analogy to illustrate what makes a good poetry meal (probably because I'm a little hungry right now), but you should feel free to use your own metaphor.

Ingredients

What ingredients are needed for a successful poem? What makes a group of words a poem? These are the questions I begin with in my writing workshops. I ask students to offer one-word answers and without fail, they begin calling out the qualities of poetry that they are familiar with. Your students may give you some of the words below, and they will also give you different words. Write them all on the board. Ask students how they define these terms. Offer hints of devices they are forgetting, or don't know yet. Feel free to share some of the definitions included here.

Brevity

Good poets express their ideas by using as few words as possible. They employ the most powerful words to convey their message to the reader. During the editing and revising process, poets look for ways to improve their writing by eliminating unnecessary material. Brevity means cutting out words that do not improve the meaning of the text, as well as substituting weak nouns and verbs with more powerful words. Consider the difference between the mouse *ran* and the mouse *scuttled* or *scampered* or *scurried*. Which do you prefer?

Conciseness

It's important to get to the point in your poetry in a straightforward way. Conciseness is like an archery contest. The goal is to get one arrow in the center of the target with the fewest shots. Organizing your thoughts effectively and using precise nouns and verbs will make your writing more concise. Brevity and conciseness are your bow and arrow. (I'm not sure if that metaphor really works, but is sounds wonderful doesn't it?)

Feeling

Speaking with feeling means that you understand the mood of the text and convey that to the reader with your voice. In our everyday lives, we all use feeling to express how we feel. Writing with feeling means that your word choice, your line breaks, and your style highlight the mood of the poem. If your poem is exciting and lively, you might choose to use bouncy, rhyming

Kwame QuickTip

The delightful writing guru Christine Hale (2013) admonishes us to favor precise nouns over generic; for example, consider the standard noun *house*. While it's short and familiar, might we think of a more potent and precise substitute such as *bungalow, cottage*, or *duplex* (depending on the image we have in our heads and what we're striving to describe)? Strong verbs follow similar rules. Do we *eat* a sweet nectarine or do we *devour, gobble*, or *inhale* this delectable stone fruit?

Invite your students to become "word detectives" and keep track of all the fabulous strong verbs and nouns they encounter in their reading, through mass media, or in the world outside the classroom. Consider creating word walls that feature synonyms for old standbys such as *house*. Do you live in a *house* or in an *A-frame*? In a *manor* or a *shack*? A *Victorian* or a *hacienda*? Learning to use and control strong, precise language begins with becoming conscious of it.

words, along with short, quick phrases. A sad poem, however, might use longer phrases and more serious words to convey the message.

Figurative Language

Sometimes we use words and phrases in ways that are different from their literal meanings. Poets use metaphor, simile, personification, alliteration, hyperbole, and onomatopoeia to make interesting comparisons between objects and situations. The effective use of figurative language allows readers to use their imaginations. It is much more interesting to describe clouds as cotton candy than as condensed water vapor hovering in the sky. The use of figurative language also appeals to sight, smell, sound, taste, and touch to create much richer poems. To study this ingredient more, have students identify imagery language (figurative language, sensory details, and action verbs) in mentor poems. Students can record their examples on the *Imagery Chart* (page 136). (A copy of the activity for primary students is included in the digital resources.)

TEACHER RESOURCES / APPENDIX A

Annotated List of Poetry Forms

acrostic: poetry in which certain letters, usually the first in each line, form a word or message when read in a sequence

ballad: a poem that tells a story similar to a folktale or legend that often has a repeated refrain

bio: a poem written about one's life, personality traits, and ambitions

blank verse: a poem written in unrhymed iambic pentameter; The iambic pentameter form often resembles the rhythms of speech.

burlesque: poetry that treats a serious subject as humor

canzone: Medieval Italian lyric style poetry with five or six stanzas and a shorter ending stanza

carpe diem: Latin expression that means "seize the day." Carpe diem poems have a theme of living for today.

cinquain: a short poem of five, usually unrhymed lines containing, respectively, two, four, six, eight, and two syllables. Line 1 has one word (the title). Line 2 has two words that describe the title. Line 3 has three words that tell the action. Line 4 has four words that express the feeling. Line 5 has one word that recalls the title.

classicism: poetry that holds the principles and ideals of beauty that are characteristic of Greek and Roman art, architecture, and literature

clerihew: a four-line verse—and the namesake of Edmund Clerihew Bentley, who was born in 1875 and crafted the first Clerihew comprising:
• rhyming couplets of AA, BB
• a person's name as its first line
• something to say about that person
• and it should make you smile

concrete: poetry written in the shape or form of an object; also known as a shape poem

couplet: rhyming stanzas made up of two lines

diamond or diamante: a diamond-shaped poem with seven lines that describes a particular topic by using one noun on the first and seventh lines, two adjectives on the second and sixth lines, three action verbs in the third and fifth lines, and four nouns in the fourth line; It can also be used to describe two contrasting subjects.

THE RED WHEELBARROW

so much depends
upon

a red wheel
barrow

glazed with rain
water

beside the white
chickens.

—*William Carlos Williams*

Form

Poems are arranged in certain ways to convey meaning. Some poetic forms such as sonnets have set rules about meter and rhyme. Other poetic forms such as haiku have a fixed syllable count for each line. Free verse poems allow the writer to choose their own style. Like other poetic elements, poets choose the form that best suits the message they want to convey. See the *Annotated List of Poetry Forms* (pages 137–140) for more examples to share with students.

Imagination

How can we express our ideas in inventive ways? Young children often think imagination means stories of dragons and princesses. However, imagination can be used in poetry to make original observations and create inspired scenarios. Shel Silverstein was a master of using imagination in his poetry. In his poem "One Inch Tall," he explains what life would be like if you were shrunk down to the size of a big bug. Using your imagination to choose your topics and express yourself in new ways makes your poetry more interesting and more entertaining to read.

Originality

Successful poets are able to use their words to make readers see things in new ways. William Carlos Williams and Pablo Neruda were respected for their talent at turning everyday, commonplace things such as a red wheelbarrow, plums, and socks into meaningful poems. More importantly, they changed the way readers looked at the world. Admit it, after you read "The Red Wheelbarrow," you never saw another one in quite the same way.

Passion

Poets need to show their enthusiasm by writing regularly. But, they also need to write about topics that are interesting, important, and meaningful to them.

If you don't like roses, then a poem about a rose will not provide the inspiration you need to write a good poem. When you are writing, pick topics that motivate you. Read poems about those same topics as well. Poets who care about their topics and their craft are more interesting than the writers who just put the words on the page.

Repetition

Poets may repeat a sound, word, phrase, line, or stanza to emphasize an idea, create rhythm, or develop drama in a poem. The effective use of repetition can be memorable for readers and make them remember the words long after they have finished reading a poem. Using repetition in your poetry can be tricky, but it can make the difference between composing a so-so poem and writing a memorable verse that inspires readers to sing your words.

Rhyme

Explaining rhyme in a technical way is difficult but we all know what rhyme means because the first poems we heard were filled with rhymes. Often rhymes occur at the ends of lines, but poems can also have rhymes within lines, known as internal rhyme. For example, consider Edgar Allan Poe's "The Raven." In poetry, rhymes generate a pattern that is pleasant to hear. Using rhyme can improve a poem, but it can also ruin it. Be careful not to sacrifice meaning by forcing rhymes into your poem.

Rhythm

Poetry that is not free verse has a regular pattern of accented syllables and unaccented syllables, which is similar to a drum beat in a song. Even if you are writing free verse, you should be aware of the way words sound together by listening to your poem aloud.

APPENDIX A / TEACHER RESOURCES

Annotated List of Poetry Forms (cont.)

diamond or diamante: a diamond shaped poem with seven lines that describes a particular topic by using one noun on the first and seventh lines, two adjectives on the second and sixth lines, three action verbs in the third and fifth lines, and four nouns in the fourth line. It can also be used to describe two contrasting subjects.

dramatic monologue: a type of poem that is spoken to a listener. The speaker addresses a specific topic while the listener unwittingly reveals details about themselves. (also known as a persona poem)

elegy: a sad and thoughtful poem about the death of an individual

epic: an extensive, serious poem that tells the story of a heroic figure

epigram: a very short, ironic, witty poem usually written as a brief couplet or quatrain; The term is derived from the Greek word epigramma, meaning inscription.

epitaph: a commemorative inscription on a tomb or mortuary monument written to praise the deceased

epithalamium (epithalamion): a poem written in honor of a bride and groom

free verse (vers libre): a poem written in either rhyme or unrhymed lines that has no set fixed metrical pattern

ghazal: a short lyrical poem that arose in Urdu; It is between 5 and 15 couplets long. Each couplet contains its own poetic thought but is linked in rhyme that is established in the first couplet and continued in the second line of each pair. The lines of each couplet are equal in length. Themes are usually connected to love and romance. The closing signature often includes the poet's name or an allusion to it.

haiku: a Japanese poem composed of three unrhymed lines of five, seven, and five syllables, usually containing a season word

Horatian ode: short lyric poem written in two- or four-line stanzas, each with the same metrical pattern, often addressed to a friend, which deals with friendship, love, and the practice of poetry. It is named after its creator, Horace.

iambic pentameter: one short syllable followed by one long one, five sets in a row (da-DAH da-DAH da-DAH da-DAH da-DAH)

EXCERPT FROM "THE RAVEN"

Once upon a midnight dreary,
    while I pondered, weak and weary,
Over many a quaint and curious
    volume of forgotten lore,
While I nodded, nearly napping,
    suddenly there came a tapping,
As of some one gently rapping,
    rapping at my chamber door.
"'Tis some visitor," I muttered,
    "tapping at my chamber door—
Only this, and nothing more."

—Edgar Allan Poe

Definition

After you finish collecting words from students, it's time to help them write a definition of poetry (or realistic fiction, short story, persuasive essay—whatever genre your students choose to tackle). Using the words that they come up with, generate a working definition that students can use throughout the workshop to guide their writing process. Here's one I've used for students:

> *Poetry is an original arrangement of words in a concise manner that uses rhythm, form, and figurative language to express a meaningful thought or experience. It creates an emotional response by showing something significant rather than telling it.*

Putting It Together

This then becomes the standard by which each poem written in the workshop can be judged. After students have completed this exercise, I like to have them read previously selected poems aloud (such as "Harlem" by Langston Hughes, "Sick" by Shel Silverstein, or "Still I Rise" by Maya Angelou), and then discuss whether the poem has the right ingredients.

A Recap on the Ingredients

- Is it authentic? Is it sharing a truth?
- Is the poet using the best form to convey the idea? (e.g., Would the poem have been better unrhymed?)
- Did the poet use the right words? Is the diction spot on?
- Are there unnecessary small words (*and*, *a*, *the*) and punctuation?
- Does the poem contain clear and concrete imagery?

And probably the most important ingredients that help to flesh out the work and make a poem more engaging for readers:

- Does the poem evoke and show, not tell?
- Does the reader have a strong emotional (or intellectual) reaction that makes them feel or think something significant?

Two great resources can be shared with students after this discussion on the definition and ingredients of poetry: *Kwame's Ingredients of Poetry* (page 141) and *Does This Poem Have the Right Ingredients?* (page 142). (A copy of the activity for primary students is included in the digital resources.) The first is a handy reminder for students that you can share or post in your room. The second includes my definition of poetry and a checklist that students can refer to as they write poetry.

Kwame QuickTip

In first grade, I read 100 books in two months and got a really cool T-shirt that said *I Read 100 Books*. In fourth grade, I won the elementary school spelling bee (I lost in the citywide bee when I misspelled *malignant*). My eighteenth book, *The Crossover*, won a Newbery Medal (I won't say any more about this, lest the mewling begin). I like to think that each of these awards fed my literary confidence, propelled me forward in the writerly life. There are many contests and competitions that provide opportunities for your students to experience this recognition. I've been a judge for the Scholastic Art & Writing Awards and a fan of their mission, "to identify students with exceptional artistic and literary talent and present their remarkable work to the world…." Through the awards, students in Grades 7–12 receive opportunities for exhibition, publication, and scholarships. For more information, check out www.artandwriting.org.

Mini-Lessons on Key Ingredients

To get students thinking more critically and creatively about painting pictures with words, I suggest offering a few mini-lessons around some of the more technical ingredients of poetry, such as rhythm, diction, and my favorite, figurative language.

Lesson in Action

Metaphors and Similes

Metaphors and similes are to poetry what sorrow and hope are to the Blues, what salt and butter are to popcorn—They add the flavor. Used properly, they allow the writer to use a few words to say a whole lot, showcase powerful emotion, and encourage the readers to use their own imaginations and interpretations, thereby sustaining interest.

In this lesson, students advance their understanding of similes and metaphors in common language by examining the use of similes and metaphors in poetry. They will use their explorations to create their own poems using unique similes and metaphors.

Resources

- "Harlem" by Langston Hughes
- "A Red, Red Rose" by Robert Burns

Lesson

1. Introduce similes to students. A simile compares two different items by using the words "like" or "as." Emphasize that effective similes make interesting and unique comparisons. Even though the items being compared are different, they have to share some characteristic for a simile to make sense.

2. Display the first stanza of "A Red, Red Rose" by Robert Burns (see page 57) and identify the similes.

3. Find a copy of and read aloud "Harlem" by Langston Hughes.

EXCERPT FROM "A RED, RED ROSE"

O my Luve's like a red, red rose
That's newly sprung in June;
O my Luve's like the melodie
That's sweetly played in tune.

—*Robert Burns*

4. Ask students to identify the similes. In the poem, Hughes uses several similes to describe what happens to a dream deferred:

   - It dries up **like** a raisin in the sun
   - It festers **like** a sore
   - It stinks **like** rotten meat
   - It sags **like** a heavy load

5. Ask students to brainstorm topics for their own simile poems.

6. Once they have selected topics, have students begin to list traits. For example, if they choose a ball, they might list characteristics such as bouncy, red, passed around, or kicked.

7. For each trait, tell them to write a simile that describes the item:

   - bounces like a scared bunny
   - as red as a fire truck

8. Encourage students to develop their similes by adding further details. Burns, for example, wrote, "my Luve's like a red, red rose / That's newly sprung in June."

9. Have students develop their similes into rough draft poems.

10. Ask students to share their drafts with partners for suggestions about revisions.

11. Allow time for students to revise and edit their poems and prepare final drafts. Students can decorate their poems with illustrations and photographs.

Mentor Texts

Students always ask me for advice on becoming a good writer. (Check out all the *Questions for Kwame* throughout this book!) It's really a simple answer: the best way to become an effective writer is to become an effective reader—one who knows how to learn from every text consumed—who can learn not just from the content of the text, but also from its structure, word choice, flow, balance, and rhythm. As the French poet and novelist Victor Hugo once observed: "To learn to read is to light a fire; every syllable that is spelled out is a spark." To cultivate those sparks, you'll want to immerse your students in the genre they want to write. If the assignment is to create a travel guide, gather an armful of such guides and give your kids the time and space to read and examine the sort of information that is included in such a guide and how it is designed and formatted. What features do they see? Maps? Descriptions of must-see destination sites? Train and bus schedules? As students explore specific genres and particular written forms, they begin to absorb the unique features, language, and syntax of their chosen genre. Reading closely—and studying a text in this way to learn how it's put together and what makes it tick—has come to be known as using a "mentor text" (Wood 2006).

Teachers can encourage students to dive further into poetry by using mentor texts and by displaying writing and thinking processes at work. Poems can be introduced to students by reading texts aloud and soliciting input. Teachers can share their own views and explain how the mentor text could be used to generate a poem.

For example, the poem "For Those Who Don't Know What to Do with a Lake" by Mandy Coe affords teachers an opportunity to engage in thinking and writing processes with students. See page 61 for other great poetry mentor texts to use with students.

By picking an object in the classroom and asking students to describe different ways it can be used (real and imaginary), you can show the value of brainstorming and prewriting. Using the students' suggestions, demonstrate through modeled or interactive writing how some of the phrases might fit into a poem. Participating in the creation of shared poems gives students the confidence to formulate their own poems. The mentor text provides a scaffold to organize their thoughts, while allowing them to integrate their own ideas and language. Come to think of it, there is really no better poetry mentor text than a student's own poetry.

FOR THOSE WHO DON'T KNOW WHAT TO DO WITH A LAKE

Like a silver knife, use it to spread sky-butter on the land.
Tie stars on your hook and fish for clouds.
In its eye see your water-twin.
Know it as a child born of the ice-age.
Capture fish-jump sparkles; wear them in your hair.
Roll up its sheen and post it to the Sahara.
Keep its secrets secret.
Don't trust its creaking winter skin.
Dip your toe into the moon at midnight.
Use the ripples to skip with.
Pour its calm in your pocket for a stormy day.

—*Mandy Coe*

FOR THOSE WHO DON'T KNOW WHAT TO DO WITH A BREADSTICK

throw it like a football
use it as a broom handle
snap it in half
use it in a sword fight
bury it in your backyard
eat it with eggs
hold it like a stick
beat it on a drum

—*Ryan, Grade 5*

FOR THOSE WHO DON'T KNOW WHAT TO DO WITH BEEF JERKY

Buy it on sale every
Thursday eat it for dinner
every Friday take it to the prom
dance with it all night long
give it to your dad for his
birthday donate it to charity
read it a bedtime story
and cuddle it to sleep

—*Liam, Grade 4*

Solo Act: Ann Marie Stephens
Elementary School Teacher and Picture Book Author

Am I crazy for using similes with first graders? Maybe, but the results are amazing. We sit in a circle and pass around a fluffy cotton ball. I start by saying, "This cotton ball is as soft as a bunny tail." I ask the students to make their own statements using "like" or "as." I mention the word simile but I don't force it. Some kids pass, others come up with hilarious ideas such as, "This cotton ball is like the hair on my daddy's face." As a follow-up, put out a basket of miscellaneous items (fork, stuffed animal, rubber figurine, apple, and so on). Put two large index cards in the basket with "like" on one and "as" on the other. Allow your students to visit the basket throughout the day to make similes for the random objects. The cards remind them of the words to use. Leave out blank cards as well so students can write their similes for others to read. They quickly get the hang of it.

Read the poem, "For Those That Don't Know What to Do with a Breadstick" by fifth grader, Ryan (page 59). Give a visual by displaying a picture of a breadstick (some kids won't know what one is), bringing in a real breadstick, or even buying enough for everyone to have their own (be aware of food allergies). Encourage students to share any new ideas to add to the poem. Tell them they are going to write a shared poem. Pick a popular topic, such as pizza or ice cream, and then brainstorm other uses for their choice. Write everything on chart paper or the board. Show how their ideas (as they accumulate) are becoming a poem. If they have too many ideas (which definitely happens), you can make multiple poems with the same title. Type them when you're finished and send everyone home with copies to share. You might even choose to save one for a "poem in your pocket." To extend this activity, put paper at your writing center with the heading "For those who don't know what to do with a ____." Write random ideas on small scraps of paper or cards and drop them into a jar or empty fishbowl. Set these ideas next to the papers. Your students can fish out topics to create their own poems if they are short on original ideas.

Recommended Poetry Mentor Texts

Among the pages of these books are countless poetry mentor texts—standalone poetry collections, anthologies, picture book poems, verse novels. Be sure your classroom library includes books such as these so students see verse in many different forms.

Grades K–2

- Alexander, Kwame. *Acoustic Rooster and His Barnyard Band*.
- Alexander, Kwame. *Animal Ark*.
- Brown, Calef. *Polkabats and Octopus Slacks*.
- Frost, Robert. *Stopping by Woods on a Snowy Evening*.
- Giovanni, Nikki. *I Am Love*.
- Hughes, Langston. *Sail Away*.
- Lewis, J. Patrick, and Douglas Florian. *Poem-mobiles: Crazy Car Poems*.
- McKay, Elly. *If You Hold a Seed*.
- Muth, Jon J. *Hi, Koo!: A Year of Seasons*.
- Myers, Walter Dean. *Harlem*.
- Singer, Marilyn. *Mirror Mirror: A Book of Reverso Poems*.
- Various authors. *In Daddy's Arms I Am Tall*.

Grades 3–5

- Alexander, Kwame. *Booked*.
- Alexander, Kwame, Chris Colderley, and Marjory Wentworth. *Out of Wonder: Poems Celebrating Poets*.
- Creech, Sharon. *Love That Dog*.
- Giovanni, Nikki (ed.) *Hip Hop Speaks to Children: A Celebration of Poetry with a Beat*.
- Greenfield, Eloise. *Honey, I Love*.
- Janeczko, Paul (ed.) *A Poke in the I: A Collection of Concrete Poems*.
- Kennedy, Caroline (ed.) *A Family of Poems: My Favorite Poems for Children*.
- Lewis, J. Patrick (ed.) *National Geographic's Book of Animal Poetry: 200 Poems with Photographs That Squeak, Soar, and Roar!*
- Sidman, Joyce, and Rick Allen. *Winter Bees & Other Poems of the Cold*.

Grades 6–8 and above

- Alexander, Kwame. *The Crossover*.
- Alexander, Kwame. *Crush: Love Poems for Teenagers*.
- Alexander, Kwame, & Mary Rand Hess. *Solo*.
- Alexander, Kwame. *Rebound*.
- Collins, Billy (ed.) *Poetry 180: A Turning Back to Poetry*.
- Grimes, Nikki. *Bronx Masquerade*.
- Hesse, Karen. *Out of the Dust*.
- Holt, K. A. *Rhyme Schemer*.
- Kennedy, Richard (ed.) *Selected Poems by e. e. cummings*.
- Hughes, Langston. *Selected Poems of Langston Hughes*.
- Nye, Naomi Shihab. *A Maze Me: Poems for Girls*.
- Smith, Hope Anita. *The Way a Door Closes*.
- Woodson, Jacqueline. *Brown Girl Dreaming*.

WHEN

the world is not so beautiful
the flowers waste water

the women can no longer find their song
the children refuse to play

there are no men to teach to love
the ground inside collapses

the coldest winter screams
the summer burns red

the sea is full of the blues
and the sky opens up

at least I'll have poetry:
a get-together of emotions

ideas with wings
words that soar.

—*Kwame Alexander*

The Rules (and How to Bend Them)

The smell of my grandmother's kitchen was an obsession of mine. Each and every Sunday, I barely sat, restless, in church, waiting to get to her house for a little piece of heaven in the form of soft-buttered rolls. After she passed away, I was unable to duplicate her recipe exactly, since according to my aunt, "There was no recipe, she simply used a little bit of this ingredient and a little bit of that one." Over the years, I made countless failed attempts to guess those exact ingredients. Eventually, I was successful at baking a recipe that at least tasted good, even if it wasn't my Granny's. Your students will fare far better than I did. They now have the ingredients to prepare a poem for publication.

Miles Davis once said, "Sometimes you have to play a long time to be able to play like yourself." Another way of saying this is that once you know the rules, you can bend or break them to create a work of art that enriches you and enthralls your audience.

Write on!

Kwame QuickTip

Once your students know the rules, it's okay to let them break them, as long as there's a purposeful reason. I've written a few poems where I forgo capitalization and punctuation in an effort to attain a more free verse, with no grammatical or punctuation distractions. For me, the way a poem fits and sounds and looks is as important as its meaning. William Carlos Williams's "The Red Wheelbarrow" bends this same rule. While he capitalizes the title, the body of the poem is lowercase. Why he does this is a great discussion to have with your students. I do it because it doesn't give any one word more meaning or importance than another. Also, I believe that the reader is more than likely to read the poem in the way I intended.

YOU CAN TOO!

1. In what ways do you already use mentor texts in your classroom? How can you incorporate poetry into that model?

2. Which poetry ingredients do you find most difficult to teach? How might mentor texts help you introduce those ingredients to students?

3. Determine two or three ways you might use Alexander's poem, "When," as a mentor text with your students.

"IF YOU OBSERVE A WORKSHOP, YOU WILL WATCH A ROOMFUL OF PEOPLE ENGAGED IN THE ACT OF WRITING.... THE CORE OF THE WORKSHOP—THE HEART, THE MARROW—IS KIDS PUTTING WORDS ON PAPER."
—JOANN PORTALUPI AND RALPH FLETCHER

CHAPTER FOUR

Writing the Draft

Form and Structure

Remember that Sting concert I was telling you about? Well, when he finally came out on stage, we were ready for him. The crowd roared. And, when he sang "ROX-anne," we joined in, fully immersed in the magical evening that lay before us. The same is true for our students. Armed with a healthy desire to express themselves on paper, and the tools with which to do this, it is now time to expose them to the various types of poetry. Some will be familiar, others new, but all are vehicles—diverse in form and function—we can use to help us navigate the writing workshop.

Again, I believe that poetry is the most powerful tool to energize student enthusiasm in writing workshop. Even children who struggle with narrative or expository tasks find success with poetry writing. Part of the reason why poetry begets success is that the range of poetic forms provides students many opportunities to experiment with language and express themselves in unique ways that are not as restrictive as other forms of writing.

Begin this phase of the workshop by asking students to name as many different forms of poetry as they can. List them on the board. Expound upon the forms named, have the students define them, read aloud examples of some of the forms mentioned, and offer forms students may not be familiar with. Use the *Annotated List of Poetry Forms* in the Appendix as a reference (pages 137–140).

Borrowed poems, haiku, clerihew, list, rhyme, and spine poems lend themselves very well to building self-assurance in student writers, primarily because the poems are fun to compose, short in nature, have very specific ingredients (syllabic structure, number of lines, rhyme scheme, etc.) that offer clear direction, and most students think they are easy to learn and apply. I say *think* because at first glance, these poems look simple enough, with lots of white space, and even though they may not be, we are interested in getting students off to a comfortable, cool, and confident start in writing workshop. The means may be a little tricky, but the ends are quite magical.

As teachers, it is our goal to pan for gold—golden lines and golden moments. This is a unique opportunity to mine for the things below the surface—aware that there is satisfaction in the work. It's time for students to apply the poetry lessons they've learned thus far, learn some new forms, and spin gold. Whether you're sitting in a chair, in a circle, or at a table, get comfortable. It's a jam session, and in true jam session style, collaboration is the key. The best teachers of writing are also writers themselves.

This section includes Lessons in Action for strong poetic forms to introduce poetry to students. For more lessons about poetic forms, check out the *Poetry Form Mini-Lessons* in Appendix B (pages 144–171)!

Solo Act: Ann Marie Stephens
Elementary School Teacher and Picture Book Author

Spine poems are a dream for younger kids. Pull out familiar hardback picture books but don't be afraid to throw in a few new titles especially if they are funny or unique. Put all the books on the floor. Pick up one and point to the spine. Have your students feel their own backbones (spines) on their bodies. Make comparisons to a book spine. Pass out sentence strips or strips of paper long enough to fit a title. Ask each student to choose one book and write the title on his or her strip of paper. Then, depending on your class size, place students into teams. Show them how they can arrange and stack their titles in any order to make poems. The poems might be nonsense and silly but always really fun and cool. (Make sure to take pictures of the stacked titles.) Once the order is chosen, let students walk around and read all the poems. Afterward, collect the strips and put them out as a Create a Spine Poem Center. Include paper in case someone creates a poem he or she would like to take home.

Spine Poems

There are two types of spine poems. The first is where you take several books and lay them on top of one another, spines facing outward, and create a poem using the titles on the spines. The other spine poem is a new type of poetry where you write the title of a book or song in a vertical line. That gives the "spine" of the poem you're about to write. Then, you write your poem (it can be about anything). The beginning of each line must start with the word in the title that's listed there.

Lesson in Action

The Spine Poem

I was facilitating my first writing workshop with second and third graders, and while they were eager to write poetry and publish a book, I struggled to come up with a plan to get them to write a publishable poem—in one day. I needed to get their skills to match their enthusiasm, and I needed to do it fast. I needed to build their confidence so they believed without a doubt that they could produce a well-crafted poem that followed the ingredients. I began with a spine poem.

To say the students, working in groups of four, had fun running around the library pulling books off the shelf, shifting them around, and trying to compose poems that made sense, is an understatement. (I'm sure the librarian didn't have quite as much fun putting the books back on the shelf.) In about 15 minutes, each group composed a poem, shared it with the class, and we were off to a rollicking start. We used this first spine poem as a building block in our workshop, and eventually worked our way up to writing more complex and challenging poems.

**KwameTime
Video for Students
*Introducing
Spine Poems***
(See page 19.)

POEMS IN THE ATTIC

<u>Poems</u> are sunlight
<u>In</u> our backyard
<u>The</u> light in our
<u>Attic</u>.

—*Kwame Alexander*

THIS IS JUST TO SAY

I have eaten
the plums
that were in
the icebox

and which
you were probably
saving
for breakfast

Forgive me
they were delicious
so sweet
and so cold

—*William Carlos Williams*

Borrowed Poems

Borrowed poetry is a type of poem that is created by "borrowing" lines or phrases from other sources, in particular poems. Borrowed poetry pays tribute and brings new life and added depth to the words of others. Students absolutely love writing these forms of poems, because, on the surface, it appears as though they don't have to do any real thinking. *Au contraire*!

While you can borrow words from newspaper articles, novel passages, signs, etc., for the purpose of this lesson, try using poetry. We've spent a great deal of time talking about listening and reading and watching great poetry, so let's build on that. And, what better poem to begin with than with a poem by Pulitzer Prize-winning poet William Carlos Williams.

Williams was a student at Horace Mann High School when he decided to become both a doctor and a writer. He established his medical practice in 1910, and he wrote poems and practiced medicine in Rutherford for the next 40 years. Inspired by the world of his patients, he wrote on prescription pads and between patient visits. He explored new forms of poetry that were completely unique by experimenting with meter (the basic rhythmic structure in a line of poetry) and enjambment (the continuation of a single thought from one line to another). Williams wanted his poems to mimic the kind of American language that he heard in everyday conversations.

One of my favorite poems, and one of Williams's most famous poems, which students and teachers love to mimic, is "This Is Just To Say." I love this poem because of its simplicity, but also because of its ... sensuality. That's right, in my estimation, this marvelous imagist poem is about as sexy as Stan Getz's sax on "Desifinado" or Etta James's bluesy contralto on "Till There Was You." But, for the purposes of your students and this lesson, let's just focus on the missing plums.

**KwameTime
Video for Students**
*Introducing
Borrowed Poems*
(See page 19.)

Lesson in Action

Borrowed Poems

When I teach poetry to elementary and middle school students, I almost always begin by reading and discussing "This Is Just To Say." Sometimes, students are unimpressed, and the boldest ones express reservations about whether this poem follows the right "ingredients." After discussing why it may or may not be poetry, I offer them this simple insight. Poetry is different from other types of writing because of the way it is written. More importantly, good poetry changes the way the reader sees the world. It can be so powerful that the reader is permanently changed after reading the poem.

"This Is Just to Say" encourages students to explore their connection with the world (Koch 1990; Sidman 2007). After reading the poem together, ask students what features of the poem stand out. At first, students may need some prompting to understand that the poem is a note left on the refrigerator. Use the following questions to guide a discussion about the poem:

- Who is the speaker?
- What is the setting?
- Who do you think the author is apologizing to?
- How would you describe the tone of this poem?
- Do you think the author is really sorry? Why?

The next step is to encourage students to make connections with the poem by sharing personal experiences:

- What kinds of things have you been sorry for?
- Tell about a time you have apologized without meaning it.

THIS IS JUST TO SAY

I have eaten
the cookies
that were in the jar.

And which you were
probably saving
for dessert.

Forgive me
they were
so scrumptious,
so colorful
and sugary.

—*Marisol, Grade 3*

Almost every one of your students will identify a time they did something that was wrong but was really fun. Because the poem is written in a personal voice, students are eager to share their stories. This is a good time to allow them to recite their experiences to partners—working out the details and emotions. Ask the students to think of times they did things they weren't supposed to, but that were really a lot of fun. Remind them to picture the scenes and to describe the settings, the feelings they experienced, and who they would apologize to.

THIS IS JUST TO SAY

I have intercepted
your pass
at Super Bowl XLI

which you probably
expected
to go for a touchdown

forgive me
it was a bad throw
and the wind was against you
and I took it to the house

it was so fulfilling
and I felt on top of the world
doing my dance in the end zone

—*Addison, Grade 6*

Using "This Is Just To Say" as a model, have students quick-write for 10 to 20 minutes about their experiences. They can then select interesting phrases and words from their quick-writes to write their own apology poems. There is always great enthusiasm for this lesson because it allows students to explore exaggeration, humor, and silly situations (Ontario Ministry of Education 2009). This experience helps writers develop an awareness of voice—some whimsical, some more serious, all valuable—and word choice, while inferring the feelings of the reader.

The results of this exercise vary from student to student. Some make insightful observations and connections between images and ideas immediately, while others need additional prompting. Before moving on, however, have students share their poetry in small groups and with the class. Sharing creates a sense of pride in and enthusiasm for their poetry, and it gives them the confidence to move on to other poems (Kovalcik and Certo 2007). Even the students who struggle with the exercise acquire understanding and insight from talking about and sharing poetry.

List Poems

List poetry is a way to focus on the message without the restrictions of rhyme, rhythm, or syllable count. Successful poetry experiences give students opportunities to define their relationships with the world, as well as to become perceptive writers. Sometimes, focusing on expression rather than specific formulas or rules grants children the opportunity to use poetry to clarify their thoughts in poignant ways.

Our lives are inundated with lists—Christmas lists, homework lists, playlists, shopping lists, to-do lists, top-five lists, and many others. For example, here is my top-five lists of poems to introduce students to poetry during your writing workshop:

- "Sick" by Shel Silverstein
- "Onomatopoeia" by Eve Merriam
- "Cloud" by Sandra Cisneros
- "Ego-tripping" by Nikki Giovanni
- "Ten Reasons Why Fathers Cry at Night" by Kwame Alexander (Poetic license, folks!)

Some of the most memorable poems are based on lists. "If I Were in Charge of the World" by Judith Viorst is a collection of the things the author would do if given the chance to make all the rules. "Sick" by Shel Silverstein is an inventory of ailments suffered by Peggy Ann McKay to avoid school. (Check out this wonderful video of the poem: www.youtube.com/watch?v=K8owqb_QLyQ.)

However, list poems are more than just inventories of things. They develop from careful selection of different possibilities. List poems often begin with a series of lines that establish a context. The ending of the poem usually focuses on a significant idea that brings closure to the text and conveys a lesson for the reader. List poems may also incorporate devices from the poet's toolbox, like alliteration, onomatopoeia, and rhyme. Eve Merriam's poem, "Onomatopoeia," is a list of sounds that originate from a rusty spigot, while "Bleezer's Ice Cream" by Jack Prelutsky is an example of a list poem that makes extensive use of rhyme.

Why Teach List Poems?

In addition to being derived from a common form of communication, list poems have a long tradition in literature. Homer's "Iliad" features lists throughout the poems of the Trojan War. Walt Whitman relied on lists in much of his poetry, including his famous poem "I Hear America Singing" where he catalogs American people in their different roles.

TEN REASONS WHY FATHERS CRY AT NIGHT

Because fifteen-year-olds don't like park swings or long walks anymore unless you're in the mall.

Because holding her hand is forbidden and kisses are lethal.

Because school was "fine," her day was "fine," and yes, she's "fine." (So why is she weeping?)

Because you want to help, but you can't read minds.

Because she is in love and that's cute, until you find his note asking her to prove it.

Because she didn't prove it.

Because next week she is in love again and this time it's real, she says her heart is heavy.

Because she yearns to take long walks in the park with him.

Because you remember the myriad woes and wonders of spring desire.

Because with trepidation and thrill you watch your daughter who suddenly wants to swing all by herself.

—*Kwame Alexander*

List poems are accessible and offer a range of entry points for students. Even the youngest children are capable of putting together a list of things organized by a topic or a question. This universality enables success because children (and adults) can develop ideas that might be inaccessible otherwise.

When my daughter was 15, she came home from school one day and announced that she wanted to go to the movies. On a date. (This was horribly shocking to me as I'd always envisioned that she wouldn't date until she was 30!) After hours and days of tears and a failure to wrap my head around this crossroads in all of our lives, my wife sent me off to do what I do whenever I'm dealing with the woes of the world. Write a poem. (See "Ten Reasons Why Fathers Cry at Night.")

When developing list poems, children (and adults) have the freedom to select topics based on their experiences and interests. This feature motivates students to share their observations. The child who is reluctant to write a narrative finds inspiration in a list of soccer equipment or sounds at a basketball game.

Finally, list poems encourage consideration of important ideas and sequencing by asking the writers to present their thoughts in a meaningful fashion for the reader. Consideration of these elements facilitates an awareness of the power of words as a form of expression. Students who understand important ideas and sequencing comprehend the material they read more easily and become more aware of the way words communicate thoughts.

Everywhere you look there are things waiting to be ordered and arranged into meaningful lists. The exercise of list poetry rouses students to the possibilities of finding poetry in the morass of everyday life—creating order from chaos. Crafting lists is the perfect prescription for conquering the blank page because list poetry engages children in the practice of writing and gives them an outlet for creative expression.

Lesson in Action

List Poems

1. Begin the lesson by reading a list poem aloud.

2. Discuss why list poems are different from common lists, emphasizing poetic devices, line breaks, and word choice, as well as the practice of linking items in creative and interesting ways. Remind students that the author is using the list to convey a message or lesson to the reader. Look for items that are different, unusual, or unexpected as they may offer special insight into the author's thoughts.

3. Pick a topic or question to focus on for your poem. Then, brainstorm words and phrases related to the topic or question.

4. Use the words and phrases to write a shared list poem.

5. Model features of the list poem, including the arrangement of ideas so it communicates a message.

6. Brainstorm variations of the theme that might be interesting to write about.

7. Allow students to select their own topics and quick-write lists of related words and phrases.

WHAT TO DO WITH BLUE

spread it
on your bread
scoop it
with your finger
taste it
on your tongue
wipe it
from your chin
don't forget
share it
with your friends

—*Chris Colderley*

8. Encourage students to select the most interesting words and phrases to create original poems.

9. Ask students to rearrange the lines to highlight the central message.

Student List Poems

1. Have students think about kinds of lists they can make, such as things in the junk drawer, things I didn't do on my summer vacation, or my favorite foods. Tell each student to choose a type of list, topic, or question.

2. Allow time for students to make lists of words and phrases about their chosen topics. Encourage them to think of things that are surprising or unusual to make the poems more interesting.

3. Have them select the most interesting words and phrases to create original poems.

4. Give students time to arrange the ideas to tell stories for the readers. They should think about the main ideas that they would like readers to learn from their poems. Many list poems end with important messages for the reader.

5. When their poems are finished, print them and have students decorate them with designs and pictures.

Using Mentor List Poems

In the poem "Cloud," Sandra Cisneros uses vivid images and rich metaphors to tell a story of transformations. She illustrates how objects can be something else depending on how you look at them and where you find them. The idea of a cloud is a fruitful way to explore lists since students can imagine lots of different things they have seen in clouds, such as animals, faces, and everyday objects.

1. Using "Cloud" as a starting point, ask students to think about the hydrological (water) cycle. Review the different processes and discuss with students the different phrases that describe H_2O in the cycle.

2. Take the opportunity to emphasize the use of figurative language, especially metaphors.

3. When it is time to write, ask each student to select a person, a place, or a thing and brainstorm all the things it might be over a period of time (or during a journey). Some good topics to include in the brainstorm are listed on the next page.

CLOUD

"If you are a poet, you will see clearly that there is a cloud floating in this sheet of paper."

—Thich Nhat Hanh

Before you became a cloud, you were an ocean, roiled and murmuring like a mouth. You were the shadow of a cloud crossing over a field of tulips. You were the tears of a man who cried into a plaid handkerchief. You were a sky without a hat. Your heart puffed and flowered like sheets drying on a line.

And when you were a tree, you listened to trees and the tree things trees told you. You were the wind in the wheels of a red bicycle. You were the spidery Maria tattooed on the hairless arm of a boy in downtown Houston. You were the rain rolling off the waxy leaves of a magnolia tree. A lock of straw-colored hair wedged between the mottled pages of a Victor Hugo novel. A crescent of soap. A spider the color of a finger nail. The black nets beneath the sea of olive trees. A skein of blue wool. A tea saucer wrapped in newspaper. An empty cracker tin. A bowl of blueberries in heavy cream. White wine in a green-stemmed glass.

And when you opened your wings to wind, across the punched-tin sky above a prison courtyard, those condemned to death and those condemned to life watched how smooth and sweet a white cloud glides.

—*Sandra Cisneros, 8.10.91, San Antonio*

Lesson in Action (cont.)

Brainstorm Topics

- a child—going to school or using his or her imagination to play
- a leaf
- a piece of paper
- a rock
- an adult—working, parenting, and so on
- money changing hands

4. Have students quick-write for 20 minutes, compiling lists of phrases.

5. Tell students to select interesting phrases and words and use them to write poems along the lines of "Cloud."

A PENNY'S TRAVELS

You were a penny in someone's pocket.
You were a skydiver without a parachute.
You were a wheel rolling down the street.
You were a person getting kicked by a monster.
You were an airplane flying in the sky.
You were a heli crashing into a sewer.
You were a swimmer swimming in the ocean and popping for breath.
You were a fish washed up on an island.
You were a bowling pin getting hit by a bowling ball.
You were someone's grave laying underground and people there singing for you.
You were a penny and always will be.

—*Ranbir, Grade 4*

Haiku

A Haiku is simple. It is about a contained moment in time. It is about being in the moment and observing that moment. And waking up (in the Buddhist sense of that phrase). A Haiku should have a concrete image in it. A Haiku more often than not refers to nature or the season or the weather. It should capture a present moment. It should express a feeling. It should have an "aha!" moment that surprises the reader.

—Leslea Newman, Poet, Children's Book Author,
Professor of Creative Writing

Haiku is often referred to as "painting with words." It is a Japanese form of poetry that has been adapted to the English language. A haiku draws attention to experiences through careful observation. This type of poem presents things in a way that is original and novel, which leads to a new way of looking at the world.

The haiku form consists of three components:

- three lines that contain 17 syllables (5, 7, and 5)
- a "seasonal" word or phrase to describe the setting
- one image, such as a picture, that appeals to as many senses as possible

A strange old man
Stops me,
Looking out of my deep mirror.

—Hitomaro

Note that many Japanese translations do not conform to the syllable pattern of 5–7–5. In contemporary haiku, the emphasis is on encapsulating a moment with careful description rather than maintaining a syllable count of 5–7–5. According to Bruce Lansky (2014), "The essence of Haiku is the way it describes natural phenomena in the fewest number of words... That artistic effect, to me, is much more important than the number of syllables used."

The fish swim quickly
The frogs dance on lily pads
Harmonious sounds.

—Christine, Grade 7

Haiku

On one of my recent school visits, I worked with a group of students to compose a community poem. I asked them what they wanted to write about, and, since it was just before lunch, they all screamed "FOOD!" I asked them to be a little more specific and they came up with *dessert*, particularly *apple pie*.

Next, I asked them to brainstorm words—familiar and new—that were directly and indirectly related to *apple pie*. At first, they gave me pretty typical responses such as *hot*, *sugary*, *flavor*, and *sweet*. Then, they leapt outside of the box and came up with words such as *majestic*, *wafting*, *orchard*, and *lattice*.

The students generated more than 40 different words, and I wrote them on the board. Then, through interactive writing, we took the words and began to arrange them in insightful, concise, and figurative ways to come up with each line of the haiku. We only had one rule: We could not use the word *apple* or *pie* in the poem. As they'd throw out lines and phrases, I'd jot down the ones that we felt resonated, until we came up with a close-to-final version of a poem we felt worked. We crossed out words that didn't help to create a clear image. We tinkered with the words to keep the proper syllable count. We made sure our final line revealed the topic. And, we wrote a community poem, in under one hour.

Aroma Wafting
Craving, Crunch, Crumbly Crust
A Sizzling Orchard

—community haiku written by ninth graders at the Singapore American School

Kwame Time Video for Students
Introducing Haiku
(See page 19.)

How to Write a Haiku

Share the following steps with students and allow time for them to write their own haiku.

KwameTime
Video for Teachers
Model Lesson: Haiku
(See page 19.)

1. Create a mind map about an experience with five spokes for the senses: sight, sound, touch, taste, and smell.

2. Use the details to write a single sentence.

3. Check to see that you have seasonal words and sensory words.

4. Cross out words that do not help to create a clear image.

5. Write the sentence in three lines like a haiku.

6. Count the syllables in each line.

7. Tinker with the syllables and word choice to match the haiku form.

8. Publish your final copy.

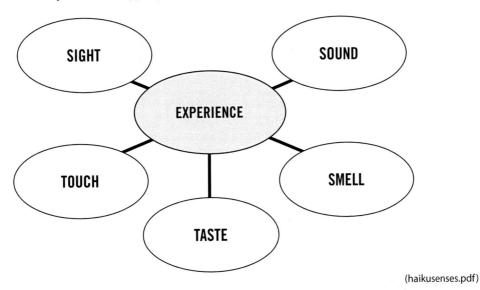

(haikusenses.pdf)

Stealing Words and Choosing a Topic

Now, that we've warmed up our writerly muse, it's time to take another step up the ladder, and focus on writing for publication (remember, our end goal is to publish). Our next step is to determine the topic or subject of the book we're going to publish. I've found that the best way to get inspired to write something of meaning is to read something of meaning. One of the ways we learn how to write good poetry, how to develop our own style, is by reading as much poetry as possible. Share with students the importance of reading in the writing process. Why does it matter? Because by reading other writers, you start to gain a greater command of the language, of vocabulary, of the limits of writing and art, of techniques and craft, and of poetry and imagination. Read for content, read for topics, and read for techniques.

Have a group discussion about what students like to read. The goal is to get students to think about their responses to literature, and then to use this as a springboard for ideas for their book. Students need to determine what subject matter their poetry book will explore. Ask them about topics that resonate with them in the books they read. Offer examples of topics and write down their suggestions. Common topics include friendship, sports, love, animals, school, and the future. We often end up with several topics that students cannot agree on, so we then make each topic a different section of the book.

Civic Action through Writing

It can be a daunting task for educators to have meaningful classroom discussions around police brutality, gun violence, a troubling political climate, and other societal ills. Yet, it's on our mind. It's on our students' minds. No matter the age of your students, they will feel the impact of current affairs. So, how do we tackle these issues and come out on the other side feeling empowered? Feeling hopeful?

I believe that writing workshop is a viable answer. When we openly explore, discuss, and write about the issues on the news, in our streets, and on our minds, it inspires us to make change. When each student has the opportunity to find their voice, share their voice, and ultimately raise their voice for what's right, dealing and healing happens.

Poetry allows us to take the heavy, emotionally weighty things happening in our world and digest them and process them. Reading a poem such as "Before I Was a Gazan" by Naomi Shihab Nye helps us to understand how a child feels when her heritage and humanity is questioned. Reading a poem such as "Still I Rise" by Maya Angelou shows us how we can never allow anyone to determine or question our humanity. Reading and writing poetry can inspire, inform, and prepare us to *write* our world.

Once you've conjured the communal muse and determined the topic(s) of your publication, it's time to "do the write thing." I usually allow students to write in any poetic form they are comfortable with (most write in free verse, some will try to sneak by with a borrowed poem—which is okay—and all must employ as many ingredients of poetry as they can).

Before they begin writing their poems for publication, I usually model writing a haiku, and then have everyone independently compose one. (See pages 78–79 for a model lesson.) The reason for this is twofold:

- At this stage, most students are beginning to see, think, and feel like writers, and they possess the confidence to write a well-crafted, short-form poem such as haiku.

- If a student writes a final poem for publication that does not "stand up" on the page, does not incorporate enough ingredients, or is more "tell" and less "show," I know I will at least have a haiku that is publishable for that student. And, it is CRUCIAL that every student have at least one quality poem that "behaves" in the publication.

Lights! Camera! Action!

When poetry is interesting and interactive, we can all find a little joy between the lines. What better way to express that joy than by giving everyone an opportunity to share his or her masterpiece? Yes, it's time to let your students share their work with each other. Some will be funny, others will employ figurative language, and some will be full of clichés. It's all good, regardless, because we've achieved our mission: Immediate and intentional immersion in interesting poetry (like that alliteration, do you?). Encourage and congratulate each student for his or her effort and product. You have just laid the foundation for an appreciation of poetry that will make your job (and theirs) that much more powerful. Not to mention, they've got a poem ready for publication. Well, not exactly ....

YOU CAN TOO!

1. In what ways can you ensure your students feel comfortable writing different forms of poetry?

2. What topics might your students be interested in writing about? How can you connect your writing workshop to students' lives outside the classroom?

"I LOVE THAT PART; THAT'S THE BEST PART, REVISION. I DO IT EVEN AFTER THE BOOKS ARE BOUND! THINKING ABOUT IT BEFORE YOU WRITE, IT IS DELICIOUS."
—TONI MORRISON

CHAPTER FIVE

Revising Is Re-Envisioning

Revision involves reflection and rethinking not what a piece of writing is, but what it might become. It requires time to consider roads not traveled in the first draft. It often involves collaboration and discussion. It can include sticky notes, index cards, computerized comments, colored pencils, highlighters, and messes. Always messes. And always allow time.

—Kate Messner

If you ask teachers, they will tell you that revision is one of the most difficult tasks to get students to perform regularly. Some of the children struggle so much to complete the assignment, they are happy to get it finished. Other children have basketball, swimming, or dancing three evenings a week and are not very interested in performing a thorough revision. Even the most eager and enthusiastic writers are ready to move on to something new once they have completed a draft. Convincing them that good writing requires extensive revision can be onerous. The good news is that poetry, with its nuance, sensory engagement, and attention to language, can help you make the case.

KwameTime
Video for Teachers
Revising Poetry
(See page 19.)

One Size Does Not Fit All

Revision encompasses a range of different elements, including capitalization, word choice, organization, and content. Even the simplest revision checklist is likely to have 5 to 10 items. Simple revision can include looking to see if the text makes sense, if the grammar and spelling are correct, and if the use of words is effective. The task of revision can seem so overwhelming that it becomes an exercise that students and teachers want to avoid.

We must keep in mind that revision is not a one-size-fits-all lesson. Some students need assistance with word choice, while others struggle with structure and organization. Conferences and small-group instruction can help develop revision skills, but there is only a limited amount of instructional time. In truth, revision is like trying on a bathing suit—at some point you have to go into the changing room and put it on by yourself.

When students ask me what's the hardest part of writing, I answer, starting, getting it all out on paper—every last forced, dissatisfying word. My favorite part is the rewriting. It's more tedious and takes the longest, but there is something satisfying about cleaning up your work, putting a polish on it, making it shine.

I wrote *Acoustic Rooster and His Barnyard Band* in two weeks, and it was a very rough draft. It took me six months after that to get it right, and I was very pleased with the outcome. *The Crossover* took me nine months to compose the first draft and about four more years of editing, rewriting, and peer review to get it in its final shape. I not only prefer rewriting to writing, but like Ms. Morrison, I love it. I think this has to do with the fact that I am a poet.

Poetry is a tool that can encourage and instill good revision habits. Poetry is usually short. The compactness of the genre allows students and teachers to read through the text several times and focus on specific aspects for improvement. It is much easier to read through a haiku or a short free-verse poem and make suggestions than it is to work through a two-page report. At the same time, in a poem, students can see almost immediately how revision can improve the quality and presentation of their work. Changing one word or including a line break can make quite a difference.

In poetry, revision has some twists that are different from prose. For example, capitalization, spelling, and syntax matter until you read e. e. cummings. In the poem "2 shes," he joins unrelated words and splits words at the ends of lines.

Emily Dickinson frequently employed dashes to punctuate her poems instead of using periods and commas. She even applied capitals to words mid-sentence and not just at the beginnings of lines.

EXCERPT FROM "2 SHES"

I
start
ed
laughing obvicouldn't
ouslyhelp it why be
cause. (9–16)

—*e. e. cummings*

Purposeful Revision

Given the examples from Cummings and Dickinson, poetry revision is not a straightforward set of rules that can be listed on an anchor chart at the front of the classroom. The most important aspect of revising poetry is being purposeful. In my workshops, I tell students they are free to ignore capitalization, make up words, or skip punctuation, but they must have a reason and intent. This restriction allows students some flexibility to exercise their creativity, but it forces them to be purposeful in the application of unconventional practices.

KwameTime
Video for Students
RE-vising Your Poems
(See page 19.)

Line Breaks

Another twist to revising poetry involves the use of line breaks. In some cases, the rule is straightforward. A haiku has 5 syllables in the first line, 7 syllables in the second line, and 5 syllables in the last line. In other cases, the placement of line breaks is less obvious. Should each line express a complete thought or image? Should each line end with a rhyme? Or, should the poet employ enjambment—continuing a thought over two lines? The idea of purpose cannot be discarded when considering where a line break should occur.

Having said this, I am honest with students when talking about line breaks. Sometimes the line breaks are based on a rule as in haiku, sometimes they are based on complete thought or a rhyme, and sometimes they are just a feeling.

QUESTIONS for KWAME

When you're stuck how do you know how to turn it around and write?
When I have writer's block, I stop trying to turn it around. I just put it aside, and work on something else. And read. Or shoot hoops with my kid. Or listen to music. Or read other people's poetry for inspiration. And, it works. Eventually, I'll get unstuck and find my way back to it.

Lesson in Action

Helping Students Understand Line Breaks

One exercise to help students understand line breaks involves "The Red Wheelbarrow" by William Carlos Williams. Begin by taking the original poem and rewriting it like prose:

So much depends upon a red wheel barrow glazed with rain water beside the white chickens.

Then ask the students to add line breaks to turn the sentence into a poem. The lesson reinforces the idea that poetry is different from prose, and it also forces students to think about the application of line breaks. In the original poem, Williams has four stanzas of two lines. The second line in each stanza has two syllables, while the first lines switch between three and four syllables. After students have presented their work and you have examined the original, ask them to decide how Williams used line breaks. You might even reflect on which students were closest to Williams's original poem.

Another exercise to help students apply line breaks is an exercise called "The Power of Three." Simply put, write a poem (or revise an existing one) with only three words in each line. (See Chris Colderley's Solo Act on page 88.)

A third exercise is to have students study the same text shared as both prose and verse to determine how line breaks affect the power of a piece. In "A Shattered Wall," the student poet added key line breaks and formatting to increase the power of her words.

A SHATTERED WALL

Sometimes, I feel like my temper and I are standing on opposite sides of a glass wall. Every time I get annoyed, my temper punches the wall, and it cracks. A tiny crack, but enough to make it easier next time I get frustrated. Sometimes, after a lot of punching, the wall shatters. I can't prevent the wall from shattering, but I can pick up the pieces and build a new one.

—Kiley, 3rd grade

A SHATTERED WALL

Sometimes, I feel like my **TEMPER** and I
are standing on opposite sides
of a **glass wall**.
Every time I get **annoyed**,
my temper punches the wall, and it

c   a   k
r   c   s.

A tiny crack, but enough
to make it *easier* next time I get frustrated.
Sometimes, after a lot of punching, the wall

s
h
a
t
t
e
r
s.

I can't **prevent** the wall from shattering,
but I can

up
pick   **the pieces** and
build
a
new
one.

Solo Act: Chris Colderley
Elementary School Teacher, Book-in-a-Day Poetry Fellow

During Kwame Alexander's Book-in-a-Day writing fellowship in Brazil, I wrote this short piece in my journal:

LOOKING FOR A MORNING SONG

In the morning I walk down the soft red sand path. Birds caw from hiding places along the way. The road ends at a clearing edged by dense palms and dark shadows. The ocean inhales and exhales somewhere past the trees. In the church on the right an organ plays. I look into the trees for the slightest movement. Maybe there's a monkey who will wave good morning before she runs away. This morning, I'm looking for a song floating in the trees.

By using the rule of three, I can apply line breaks to this piece of writing:

LOOKING FOR A MORNING SONG

In the morning
I walk down
the soft red
sand path. Birds
caw from hiding
places along the
way. The road
ends at a
clearing edged by
dense palms and
dark shadows. The
ocean inhales and
exhales somewhere
past the trees.
In the church
on the right
an organ plays.
I look into
the trees for
the slightest movement.
Maybe there's a
monkey who will
wave good morning
before she runs
away. This morning,
I'm looking for
a song floating
in the trees.

The poem is not complete yet, but I do have a piece that looks like a poem and can be revised with a purpose in mind. Have students try this with pieces of their writing. This exercise helps students with the organization of their poetry and gives them a starting point for more serious revision.

Word Choice

Another aspect of revision in poetry is word choice. Although the right word in the right place is an important tenet of prose, it is more critical in poetry.

Lesson in Action

Helping Students Understand Word Choice

"How to Ruin a Poem" (Thinkmap Visual Thesaurus 2012) is a lesson that asks students to alter a classic poem by using inelegant language and clumsy word choice. Using Gwendolyn Brooks's poem "We Real Cool" shows how this exercise reinforces word choice.

WE REAL COOL

We real cool. We
Left school. We

Lurk late. We
Strike straight. We

Sing sin. We
Thin gin. We

Jazz June. We
Die soon.

EXCERPT FROM "RUINED COOL"

We are trendy. We
Left the academy. We

Hang around after dark. We
Shoot pool. We

Say bad things. We
Drink liquor. We

Mock good things. We
Will perish in a little while.

In the "ruin a poem" revision, the brevity of the poem is lost along with the rhyme and rhythm that make it such a memorable piece of writing. The changes also remove the alliteration that Brooks used to create a firm beat, as well as the creative word choices such as "thin" and "June."

Sharing Poetry

"It is important to read your poems aloud in order to really understand them."
—Nikki Giovanni

Reading poetry aloud to a classmate or to the entire class should also be a part of the revising and rewriting process during writing workshop. Creating a classroom where students are comfortable sharing their work requires some attention to etiquette and rules of engagement.

These behaviors begin well before students make formal presentations and should be established early in the year. If you want students to share their work, you have to create a community of writers that is safe and supportive, but most of all, honest. Any serious writer knows that the world is full of critics. Students need to be taught that constructive criticism is not a personal attack, but an opportunity to reflect upon their work and make improvements.

Small-group shared reading and writing with peers is a practice that allows students to engage in meaningful dialogue about their writing and think about the choices they have made in their texts.

Kwame's Wise, Kind Student Listening Guide

- Listen, listen, listen! Shhhhhh. No talking over the poet.
- Focus. Rustling papers or moving around is a distraction. Stay put.
- Be kind to the poet. No boo-ing, eye rolling, or making fun.
- Offer applause or snaps. It takes a lot to speak in front of a group.
- Offer criticism. Start with what you liked, provide constructive criticism on what could have been better, then end with something you liked.
- Offer suggestions for possible extensions, deletions, or follow-up poems.
- Respect the mic! Be nice and do unto other poets as you would like them to do unto you.

Solo Act: Ann Marie Stephens
Elementary School Teacher and Picture Book Author

The act of revising can be a daunting task at any age, especially with young children who are still learning what this means. But we can work on word choice, especially when we combine it with the borrowed poem concept.

Choose a simple poem such as the oldie but goodie "Roses Are Red." Write the poem on a chart or the board. Circle the words red, blue, sweet, and you. Ask the students to look through their crayon boxes for red and blue crayons with unique names. (You'll get things such as lava and manatee these days!) Record the names for the class to see. Then ask for suggestions to replace the word sweet. Talk about things that are sweet, and add these to your list. Rewrite the poem by choosing a new word for each of your circled words. Read the new poem aloud. The results are usually hilarious!

Do a few more shared examples. Later, create a template with this same poem, leaving blanks for the circled words (rosespoem.pdf). Give each student a copy, and allow them to use the lists to create their own borrowed poems with amazing word choices! Some students will even want to use their own ideas. Encourage sharing when they are complete.

Literary Excellence

Time spent revising poetry teaches students to write carefully and purposely. Once students believe their personal choices have a purpose and a value, they are more eager to undertake the task of revision. All poems are works in progress. Part of the experience is giving students ownership and encouraging them to pursue the kind of literary excellence necessary for publication.

YOU CAN TOO!

1. How can you establish with your students that revision may be the most important part of the writing process?

2. For what reasons are line breaks and word choice more important with verse than with prose?

Part 2: Publishing

"Our children ... will regard themselves in a new light if they are published authors."

—Lucy Calkins

"PUBLICATION IN THE WRITING WORKSHOP SHOULD BE A GIVEN —FREQUENT AND ONGOING—AND NOT AN AWARD BESTOWED ON WHAT TEACHERS DECIDE IS THE 'GOOD' WRITING."
—NANCIE ATWELL

CHAPTER SIX

Making Student-Run Publishing a Priority

By this point, each student will have completed at least one poem that "behaves," that has the right ingredients, that they (and you) feel stands up on the page.

What better way to showcase your students' literary accomplishments than by publishing— the process of taking their work from page to proverbial stage. Now, don't let this process scare you. While publishing may seem complex (like trying to understand the sophisticated syncopation of jazz pianist Horace Silver or trying to understand what I just said), it's really a smooth, swinging process flavored with bounce and rhythm (like the bluesy melody in Silver's "Song for My Father"). Publishing is probably the least used aspect of the writing workshop in schools, but possibly the most rewarding. So, let me show you how to bring it into your classroom and, get this, let your students do most of the work!

Why Publish in the Classroom?

This writing workshop is built on the belief that students become avid readers and engaged writers when they assume responsibility for becoming authors. When students see the fruit of their labor and the response from readers, a permanent reading/writing connection is made that will transform the way they view and appreciate language and literature.

KwameTime
Video for Teachers
Why Publish?
(See page 19.)

Wendy Ramirez, a second-grade teacher who has incorporated a publishing cycle into her writing workshop, explains why she's a believer in the power of publishing.

> *Overall, I feel publishing students' work and celebrating their achievement has given them a sense of pride and ownership of their academic work that they had not realized was possible beforehand. I learned how important publishing can be to students' confidence and sense of authorship. I believe publishing should be a priority in all classrooms.*
>
> —Wendy Ramirez, 2007

Publishing also emphasizes that writing is a social process—an exchange of ideas between authors and readers, not just a performance for the teachers. Having feedback from readers provides motivation for writing and emphasizes higher-level critical thinking, creativity, and

Solo Act: Arielle Eckstut and David Henry Sterry
Coauthors of *The Essential Guide to Getting Your Book Published*

"Our daughter is 12. She has already self-published one novel and is deep into editing her second," read the email. Astonishing? Not at all. We hear this all the time. In fact, we've had kids as young as 6 come to our events and pitch us their books in front of a room full of adults. Take Katie Mishra, who was 11 when she stunned the crowd with her amazing one-minute description of her novel, Gukky Tales: The Quest for the Golden Quarter. *Katie went on to self-publish her book, was featured in her local paper, and did her first reading at the bookstore where she originally pitched us her book.*

Katie's story wouldn't have been possible even a decade ago. The publishing world has been turned upside down in recent years. And these changes mean lots of great news to current and future authors. In fact, we've come to believe that this is the greatest time in history to write a book. Today's writers have the chance to get their ideas into the hands of larger groups of people than ever before.

organization. Classroom publishing centers are becoming more prominent as teachers strive to give students authentic purposes for writing and to allow their work to be shared with others beyond classroom boundaries.

Global Teacher Prize winner and writing teacher extraordinaire Nancie Atwell says of classroom publication:

> *A sense of audience—the knowledge that someone will read what they have written—is crucial to young writers. Kids write with purpose and passion when they know that people they care about reaching will read what they have to say. More importantly, through using writing to reach out to the world, students learn what writing is good for .... It's a daily occasion for students to discover why writing matters in their lives and in others' and what it can do for them and the world.*
>
> —Nancie Atwell (1998, 498)

For hundreds of years, a book has been a bunch of words, symbols, and maybe some pictures printed on paper and bound between two covers held together by a spine. Back in the fifteenth century, printed books cost an arm, a leg, a couple of eyes, and a few brains. Now rich and poor, young and old alike are able to produce, buy, and read books. And they no longer have to rely on a small group of publishing experts to get published. Because there is now no barrier to publishing. "The opportunities for authors are boundless and growing exponentially every year," says Michael Cader, creator of Publishers Lunch and Publishers Marketplace.

As the walls have come down, the interest in getting published has gone up—especially from young people. Because they are so tech-savvy and hip to what's going on in the world, we see kids all over the country show up to our workshops with full manuscripts in hand. We also see teachers and librarians who are looking to help these young writers realize their dreams. Sometimes these dreams are to create a one-off zine. Sometimes they're to write the next Harry Potter. But for the first time in history, we can honestly say that all these dreams are possible. How exciting is that?!

Whether kids start with a bunch of poems scribbled in the margins of their notebooks, a blog featuring their thoughts of the day, or line-by-line tweets of their novels, kids can now be authors in literally minutes. If you don't believe us, just ask Katie Mishra.

Exploring Publishing Alternatives

After several years of leading Book-in-a-Day workshops in middle and high schools across the country, I was invited to bring the workshop to an elementary school in Canada. (Chris Colderley has participated in my workshop six times!) My first reaction was, "This will never work!" You see, the workshop is student run. I'm Kwame. I teach and guide the students in the writing and publishing process and let them create their own song. The process worked with tweens and teens, but surely this independent process would never work with third and fourth graders. So naturally I said "Yes!" And, here's the thing, friends, when you say yes, the students will echo you. Confidence and enthusiasm are contagious, especially with young people, who already believe they are invincible.

Over the course of five hours, the 30 elementary students came up with a title for their book (*Hatching Hope*, because they said that their poems birthed possibility—how wonderful is that!), proofread all their poems, designed a cover, ordered a bar code, wrote the dedication and the introduction, shot a promo video, and embraced the writerly life with a zeal that was awe inspiring. They believed they could do it, and they did. Their book was printed two weeks later, and they held a community-wide book signing that was attended by more than 300 people. The pride on their faces, and on their teachers' faces, propelled each of them to a higher level of engagement with literacy and literature. Since that school, I have even tackled primary grades with similar success. Just ask Ann Marie Stephens and her first graders, who have participated three times!

QUESTIONS for KWAME

Do I have to publish a book with my class?
Publishing is not mandatory. The value of studying and writing poetry in a workshop setting and sharing writing is priceless. But the sharing can be done through reader's theater, oral reports, small groups, centers, and even home sharing. Publishing has huge benefits though, as your students will be able to hold a bound book of their efforts. They can share copies of the book with family and friends. You should do what works best for you and your class.

How do/did you build an extensive vocabulary?
I read the dictionary and encyclopedia as a child. My dad had a bad case of logorrhea. Also, I do word-of-the-day at my house. I love discovering new words.

As I mentioned, I grew up in a household with a father who owned a book publishing company and employed all his children. The name of his small press was P. C. E. C. E. Book Service (I have no idea what the acronym stood for, but it sounded like PEACE when you said it. At school, my friends would ask, "Why do you answer your phone, 'Police, may I help you?'"), and he published paperback and hardcover books, which were the traditional vehicles for literature. Back then. But, I'm here to tell you: There's something else—a new world of never ending happiness. (Okay, I just mixed musical metaphors. First jazz, now Prince!) Today, there are a plethora of new technologies that make it easy to publish students' work.

Before we delve into the fine and fun art of making a book, let's take a look at some classroom publishing alternatives.

Broadsides

I may be cool, but I'm still a little old school. Publishing a broadside is a classy way to share student work with the community. A broadside is a sheet of paper or a poster with a message, story, or poem printed on one side. They were first introduced in the sixteenth century. In the Victorian era, broadsides were printed on thin sheets of paper and sold for a penny or half-penny in London. When formatting a broadside, care is given to the design, font, and point size chosen for the title and text, since it is usually framed and hung for public display.

Broadsides of your students' work can be printed, fairly inexpensively, on your printer or at the local copy shop. Typically, they are somewhat classy looking—sometimes with art incorporated—and are printed on a little heavier stock of paper, sometimes glossy. They are not only visually appealing, they're collectible. And they make beautiful gifts!

Posting broadsides on walls in the classroom, library, around the school, and online is a great way to showcase a student author's work. Having the student author sign the broadside adds a nice finish to a very classy publication.

Digital Poetry

Technology is everywhere—from watches that alert us about recent happenings to phones that are sometimes smarter than their handlers. In an age where words literally fall from birds (Twitter), nest in clouds (iCloud), snap in chats (Snapchat), supplant faces in books (Facebook), and layer by the gram (Instagram), digital poetry is a fun and relevant form of publishing. Many writers and artists are even writing books and recording albums on their phones (e.g., Drake). According to Digital Poet Jason Nelson, "In the simplest terms, Digital Poems are born from the combination of technology and poetry, with writers using all multimedia elements as critical texts. Sounds, images, movement, video, interactivity, and words are combined to create new poetic forms and experiences" (2012).

Most classrooms and media centers are outfitted with at least one laptop and/or tablet. Using this resource to access classroom publishing apps and websites is a great way to publish. Education and presentation tools, such as the applications Prezi, Canvastic, and Storybird, allow your students to publish and present their poetry, stories, and picture books in innovative ways online, while incorporating illustrations, photos, video, and text. Check out the different mobile and web-based options—many of which are free—and see which meets your needs in the most user-friendly way.

Website Showcase

Most students are used to typing up their writing with word processing tools from Microsoft, Apple, or even Google. Although these tools are definitely useful for students who move from paper to a digital platform, it doesn't have to stop there. Students can create their own websites to showcase their work and share their writing with the world.

An introduction to coding or computer science skills might be useful for students to have over the course of the school year, but it might not fit into the time you've carved out for writing. Thankfully, there are a lot of free, easy-to-use tools that make it possible for students to create websites without learning how to code. Students can take the work they've created in writing workshop; add images, videos, and links; and publish their writing for the world to see! Students are becoming increasingly comfortable reading information online and navigating websites—now it's their chance to create websites to publish their writing.

Spark Page and *Google Sites* are two examples of free website creation tools for students. Without too much guidance or support, students can create websites that show off their independent or shared writing. When they publish their websites, students will have links they can share with friends, family, or on social media for the whole world to see!

Solo Act: Monica Burns
Author of *Taming the Wild Text: Literacy Strategies for Today's Reader*

As a classroom teacher, I spent several years introducing students to persuasive writing techniques, asking them to take a position and conduct research to support their opinions. Integrating technology into the writing process started slowly as we increased our access to digital tools. One year at the conclusion of a writing unit, I was looking for a new way to share student work—an attempt to connect students with a wider audience for their writing.

Rather than using the camera on a smartphone or tablet like we might use today, I had access to a small handheld video camera to record students. Instead of requiring students to stand in front of the class to read their persuasive essays aloud, I asked students to choose a few sentences from their writing that they felt would grab the attention of a reader. Many students leaned towards the first few sentences of their writing, and they practiced reading the short sections aloud before a camera was introduced into the equation.

Each student had the chance to record their selection as they read it to the camera. I took each short clip and combined them using the tool iMovie and added soft music to the background. We were ready to share our writing with an audience.

I showed the video clip to our principal and she suggested showcasing our "persuasive writing movie" on the television screen mounted at the entrance to the school. The students were excited to see a video compilation of all their writing presented to the whole school as well as visitors! They had an instant audience and were so proud of their writing.

During my time as a classroom teacher, my access to technology increased as I participated in a one-to-one initiative. Students were soon able to share their work in screencasts, ebooks, and through cartoon animation. Although it seems simple looking back at it now, the ability to record short clips, combine them into a class video, and share them with our school community is where it all started!

Interactive eBooks

Book publishing can take many forms and students can make the most of digital tools to share their writing. An ebook has a variety of features that will vary based on the tool you and your students use for book publishing. Typically an ebook contains a combination of media such as text, video, and images. You might also find an ebook tool that lets you add hyperlinks, graphics, or comics to the pages.

A popular classroom tool for making ebooks is *Book Creator*. Students can choose to work independently or collaboratively using this tool—on both tablets or computers. When students create ebooks, they can record their own voices to narrate their stories, snap selfies for "About the Author" pages, and learn about the features present in both print and digital books. In addition to *Book Creator*, *iBooks Author* is a popular publishing tool for creating ebooks that allows students to add interactive widgets to the pages of their books.

There are many things that make interactive ebooks special for both students creating their digital stories and for readers of the texts. Students can incorporate pictures they have snapped or images they have curated and create very shareable final products. Their readers can open the ebooks on their personal devices to swipe through the pages and hear the voices of student authors.

 Kwame QuickTip

Encourage students to create visual poems using apps and websites such as Wixie, Pixie, and Animoto; watch them morph into passionate amateur filmmakers. (Getty Images has created a "How to Create a Visual Poem" video tutorial here: www.youtube.com/watch?v=wWpMB6gmBYA&feature=youtu.be). Want to really step up your game? Have them record their poems on a website such as vocaroo.com. Want to be the coolest teacher or librarian ever? Have students create QR codes at www.qrstuff.com, link them to their recordings, and then post their printed poems (with QR codes beneath), and let the scanning commence.

Solo Act: Kim Hardwick
Principal, Clayton Huey Elementary School in New York

When I was an ELA director on Long Island, I was extremely grateful that the district agreed to allow TWO groups to participate in the Book-in-a-Day workshop. One was comprised of seniors from the Advanced Placement class, and the other was a heterogeneous group of underclassmen. While I recall one group initiating the process with more confidence and motivation, you could NOT tell the groups apart by the end of the first day spent with Kwame, who knew each student's name before noon.

The workshop incorporated poetry-writing activities, which allowed students to open up in front of each other and share personal life experiences—one student sharing the loss of her mother, another sharing a personal skill of mastering the ukulele. The spectrum of emotions was vast, but it only made the experience that more intense and unforgettable for all involved. At the end of the day, each student committed to revising and submitting at least one poem, with the guidance and support of the teacher mentors who were present throughout the day.

If I thought the first workshop was impressive, the second day was mind blowing and nothing less than transformational. All aspects of the publishing process were explained, tasks were divided, teams formed, and goals were set to be completed by the end of the day.

Each component of the process was critical to the success of the final product, and I watched with amazement as the students gravitated toward jobs that they were interested in. Marketing, page/cover design, editing—each working part coming together to form the perfect whole: a published book.

Each team had its own energy and focus and yet, when the entire group needed to come together to make decisions, such as identifying a common theme or voting on a student-generated title, they were one again. A true literary team! I think they even surprised themselves with what they were able to accomplish since there are too few opportunities for true independence in education today.

Blogs

Online blog publishing with tools such as Tumblr, Blogger, and WordPress can build students' writerly confidence. Our students are already skilled and savvy in using the digital landscape to communicate. Whether on Instagram or Twitter, they are publishing regularly. Thus, using these familiar tools to create popular projects such as a class website or poetry journal can be very gratifying and simple. According to a 2013 study done by the University of Michigan's Sweetland Center for Writing, "By blogging, students can take ownership of their writing, become better observers of others' writing, and develop a more immediate and powerful understanding of audience ... Guided by clear expectations of what is required in a class blog, students can see their writing develop over the course of the term."

The writing portion of this workshop can take place over a class, a week, a month, or even a semester, but I highly recommend the publishing workshop take place in a shorter time span. While we know it can be done in a day, two to three weeks is more reasonable for most schools—and it still sets a fast-enough pace to maintain the continuity of creativity, you know, keep the rhythm.

KwameTime
Video for Students
Publishing: Put Your
Words into the World!
(See page 19.)

Creating a Classroom Publishing Center

What if you put a group of students into a classroom for one day and taught them how to craft good stories and poems—haiku, free verse, etc.—and just let them write about anything they wanted? Allowed them to express their thoughts, feelings, and ideas about their world? What if you then equipped those students with the tools to actually publish a collection of their work ... Could they then come up with a title, design a cover, proofread, write an introduction? Could they summon the focus and courage to accomplish such a lofty goal? Could we teach them to do the write thing? Could we provide a literary experience that was fun, inspirational, and transformative? Could these students produce a book?

I took my six-year-old daughter to see *The Lion King* on Broadway, and she was spellbound. The show was full of bounce and soul-stirring rhythm, and even though it was way past her bedtime, she sat on the edge of her seat for three-plus hours. (Of course, she fell asleep in the taxi on the way to the hotel, which, ironically, is what I do each time I complete the Book-in-a-Day publishing workshop!) Publishing a book in your classroom requires high energy and lots of movement. But once your students learn the basics of producing a book and get into a rhythm, the outcome is magical and profound. You will have a classroom that is transformed into a vibrant book publishing office, with editorial questions being asked and answered (Should the librarian or principal write the foreword?), technical decisions being debated and made (the footer should be centered, not left justified), and publishing tasks being assigned and carried out (we need an ISBN). This is active literacy—students engaged with, and empowered by, literature.

QUESTIONS for KWAME

How do you encourage ideas without implanting them?

One of the best strategies for encouraging without implanting is to ask questions of the writer. When they get stumped or don't know where to begin, ask questions such as, "What are you passionate about?", "How did that sound? Feel? Taste?", or "What metaphor might work here?" Reading poems like the poems you want to write is also helpful inspiration. Some students respond well to visualizing. They close their eyes and imagine their setting or their subject, and they then work that into strong sensory writing.

YOU CAN TOO!

1. For what reasons is publishing an important part of the writing process for your students?

2. What options will you offer your students for publishing their writing?

3. How can technology extend the possibilities of publishing for students?

"WHEN I WAS 6, KWAME ALEXANDER'S GUIDANCE AND COACHING NOT ONLY MADE NAVIGATING THIS WORLD MUCH CLEARER, HE ALSO OPENED DOORS OF OPPORTUNITY AND POSSIBILITY THAT LAUNCHED MY WRITING AND PUBLISHING CAREER."
—NONI CARTER, AUTHOR OF *GOOD FORTUNE: A NOVEL*, DOCTORAL STUDENT, COLUMBIA UNIVERSITY

CHAPTER SEVEN

Step-by-Step Book Publishing

There are five steps to successfully publishing an anthology of your students' work. You can spend as much time as you like on each step—or, if you're really brave, you could do it in the same way I did in seventy-six schools, over nine years—IN ONE DAY!

Step 1: Select the Poems

The responsibility of choosing the final poems for the manuscript, for the most part, rests with you, the teacher. Be sure every student has at least one piece in your finished manuscript. Some students may be disappointed because a particular poem was not included, but that's okay. We aim to provide a real-world experience for the student authors, and thus, in the real world, every author has an editor who makes the final decisions on what to include in a manuscript. You will serve this role, and use the standards and rules decided on previously to help you make these important decisions, including:

- Does the poem include the proper ingredients?
  - Does it show, not tell?
  - Does it make you feel something?

- Is the poem on theme?

- How many poems does this student have, and is there a limit?

Step 2: Produce the Final Manuscript

Ask students to gather/type all final poems in a single *Microsoft Word* document (or whatever program you use). It would be best to use the following format: left-justified, 1.5 line spacing, 12-point font size, in Courier (or other very readable) font. Remove all formatting—no boldface, underlines, etc.—except italics (which the poet may be using for emphasis). Each poem should have the title at the top of the poem and the author's name at the bottom. (I intentionally left off last names when I worked with students, but you don't have to do.)

KwameTime
Video for Students
Brainstorming a
Book Title
(See page 19.)

Step 3: Choose a Title

Watermelon Man. Salt Peanuts. I've Got You Under My Skin. Mack the Knife. What do all these have in common? They're all intriguing titles (of pretty amazing jazz songs). Like these hits, every great book needs a great title.

Remind students of the theme(s) or subject(s) of their book. Have them brainstorm and come up with ideas for titles. The idea is to come up with as many titles as possible. You should have some discussion with them about what makes a good title and give them examples. To conjure the creative

Kwame QuickTip

In more than 75 Book-in-a-Day workshops, we've seen only two instances of plagiarism, but you will want to question anything that seems like it might be taken from another source. You will also need to establish a policy concerning profanity since there will be an emotional rawness to some of the older students' work.

Solo Act: Tinesha Davis
Book-in-a-Day Publishing Coach and Author of *Holler at the Moon*

A reader will look at a title for a few seconds before making some conclusions. In those seconds, you, the author, must appeal literally to three of the five senses a person has: Sight, Sound, Taste, and then figuratively to the last two—Touch and Smell.

1. **Sight:** When someone first comes in visual contact with your book's title, it is usually by seeing it on the front cover or book spine. Your title should be aesthetically pleasing.

2. **Speech:** When reading the title aloud, if a person stumbles over the words or hesitates to say them out loud, a level of difficulty will be added in marketing the book. No matter if you are writing the book for family members and friends only or giving it away for free, there will always be an element of marketing involved. Your title should roll smoothly off the tongue.

3. **Sound:** Your title will be heard often. How does it sound? Is it as concise and clear as it could be? Is it written well?

4. **Touch:** Touch also means to "relate to" or "to have an influence on." Figuratively, your title must allow itself to touch or be touched by being relatable to your readers or having some sort of emotional influence on them.

5. **Smell:** Your title should figuratively give off an "aroma." In other words, it should project "a distinctive quality or atmosphere." If the aroma the title gives off suggests that very little thought or concern was given to it, people will assume that the rest of the book is the same way. A title should not smell like a cliché.

Write all the students' title suggestions on the board. After you've generated a ton of title ideas (I usually solicit at least 40 or so), instruct the students to show their support for each title, by applause, as you call them out. Erase titles that elicit little support. This activity is always quite fun for the students, and once you narrow it down to the top three, it can often become slightly contentious. The beauty of this is your publishing experience is beginning with intense passion and ownership. Once you have your top three titles, take a secret or public vote.

UNTOUCHABLE

I was scared of the monster.
Afraid it would find me,
Overwhelmed with sadness,
The monster was a destroyer
  of dreams
The dreams of the heart
But my heart was filled with
Love and courage.
The brilliance of my brave heart
Showed me I was untouchable.

—*Jacquelin, Grade 5*

Someone once told me
that purple Converse are the
essence of high school.

—*Nicole, Grade 11*

muse and choose a title that is relevant, catchy, and marketable to the target audience, students will need to brainstorm and perhaps even do some research. Students can view book titles (from different genres) in the classroom, school library, or online. You can then discuss and debate the merits of different titles as a class.

Step 4: Publish the Book

Just as there are specific ingredients that make a poem successful, there are similar ingredients that produce a successful book. For all intents and purposes, students are starting a publishing company, and to publish a successful book in this short amount of time, they will each be in charge of one of these ingredients. Each student should be assigned to a different "department" in the publishing company:

- **Team 1: Editorial**
- **Team 2: Proofreading**
- **Team 3: Production**
- **Team 4: Marketing**
- **Team 5: Design**

In most cases, you can allow students to choose which team they want to be on. (I actually passed out staff badges for each department, which really made students feel like responsible employees. See badges in the digital resources: badges.pdf!)

Show students one of *The Write Thing* videos or a video of an author giving a book reading or at a book signing. This will get students inspired and excited about what's in store for them.

Choose one person from each team to be a team leader and have them read their corresponding checklists. Assign different areas of the classroom or library/media center for each team. After teams are at their respective "offices," each department begins the workday.

During the writing workshop, you will float among the groups reminding students of tasks, answering questions, and providing any necessary guidance and coaching. What you'll find is that once the students get their instructions, they will be off and running, as if they've been doing this all their lives.

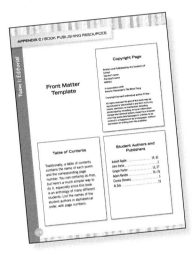

Team 1: Editorial

This group of 2–5 students is in charge of writing front matter for the book. Read and share the *Front Matter Template*, *Editorial Team Notes*, and *Editorial Checklist* on pages 172–176 for explanations of the following front matter components:

- Copyright Page
- Subtitle
- Dedication
- Foreword
- Introduction
- Epigraphs
- Acknowledgments

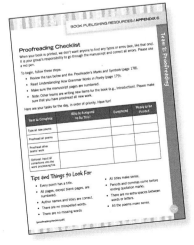

Team 2: Proofreading

This group of 2–6 students is responsible for proofreading all the poems and front matter in the book—checking for typos, misspelled words, formatting (e.g., footers are in place). In the case where there is a question about clarity or content, the proofreader should consult the author before making a change. Read and share the *Proofreading Checklist* and *Proofreading Marks and Symbols* on pages 177–178. This team will also benefit from reading *Understanding How Grammar Works in Poetry* (page 179).

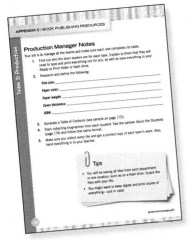

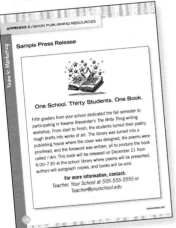

Team 3: Production

This group of 1–2 students is responsible for managing the other groups, making sure all items are completed in a timely manner, gathering/fine-tuning biographies of each student author, choosing paper, and working with you to place the initial printing order. Read and share the *Production Manager Notes* and *Production Checklist* (pages 180–182).

Team 4: Marketing

This group of 6–8 students is in charge of all marketing and promotional aspects of the book:

- Planning the book launch party
- Creating flyers
- Researching media alerts
- Writing media alerts
- Writing a blog
- Documenting the day in photographs and/or video

This is often the loudest and rowdiest group. Read and share the *Marketing Checklist*, *Book Party Form*, *Sample Press Release*, and *Video Checklist* on pages 183–187.

Team 5: Design

This group of 2–6 students is tasked with determining the size of the book, known as the "trim size" in publishing circles. I've noticed that the older the students, the more likely they are to choose odd-shaped sizes. I like to stay simple and encourage a standard size, such as 5.5" x 8.5", 7" x 10", or 8" x 11". The Design team will also choose the font that is used for the layout of the book's interior. They will brainstorm cover concepts and make mock-ups of the book cover for students to review. I've saved this group for last, as it requires a technical and artistic savvy that only a few students will have. (I sure didn't!) It is often the most desired team, so it's good to have an idea of which students might best serve this undertaking.

Out of the 76 schools in which I led the Book-in-a-Day workshops, only 10 of the books were actually designed in full by students. That was because teaching, coaching, and guiding students in such a technical assignment requires much more time than the five hours allotted. Choosing a font and layout for the interior of the book is a bit easier than designing a cover, though it is more tedious. Most students should be able to complete the interior design—the cover is a different story.

KwameTime
Video for Teachers
*Setting Up
Your Classroom
Publishing Teams*
(See page 19.)

In the situations where the cover was designed, wholly, in the workshop, the students were either graphics/illustration wizards, or, and this was very rare, the school had a graphics department. Once you have a few concepts, much like in the title process, students should vote on the "best" cover. That concept is then given to a designer who can work their magic to produce a final cover.

Read and share the *Design Checklist*, *Guide to Book Cover Design*, *Image Selection Form*, and *Guide to Interior Design* on pages 188–192. For further help in guiding this team on their massive tasks, check out the *Interior Layout Mini-Lesson* (page 193).

Kwame QuickTip

Inevitably, the students are going to come up with some hilarious and strange titles. One group I worked with came up with "?!" to which I then asked, "How are you going to pronounce the title?" Another group wanted their title to be in Morse code. Be prepared to encourage creativity, while also helping them stay true to the purpose of having a title that readers can connect to. One-word titles seem to work the best for these books.

Where Do I Find a Designer?

Unless you or a colleague are closet graphic designers, I offer the following suggestions for putting the finishing design touches on the students' book:

- Use an online cover design tool (see Step 5 for details) and do it yourself.

- Find a student at a local art school or college who is willing to work *gratis* for experience and/or credit.

- Hire a freelance designer through an online service such as Upwork. These services are usually quite inexpensive, and you can browse portfolios of freelancers until you find the right match. Or, just contact Jana (she's done countless Book-in-a-Day books) at www.impactstudiosonline.com and tell her a handsome poet sent you.

Step 5: Explore Printing Options

If you plan on publishing a small number of books ... you'll definitely want to explore Print-on-Demand. And you'll have many providers to choose from. There are companies that simply print ... and companies that offer "author services."

—Arielle Eckstut and David Henry Sterry,
The Essential Guide to Getting Your Book Published

With all the new technologies (e.g., ebook, print-on-demand), this step just may be the easiest of all. The process of getting your files fine-tuned and printed is inexpensive and accessible.

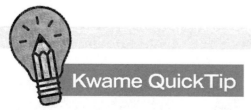

Kwame QuickTip

It's important to bring everyone back together for one to two staff meetings during the course of putting the book together to discuss how things are going, have students share what they are doing, and talk about next steps. This will help ensure that all deadlines are met.

Kwame QuickTip

To help you compile your book, I've included full manuscript examples (interiors and covers) in the digital resources for this book (examplemanuscript.pdf). See page 207 for more information. Seeing the work done by another class will help you and your students put the finishing touches on your book!

Ebooks are definitely the fastest growing segment of publishing, but it's still nearly impossible to surpass the thrill a student feels when he or she holds her own published book in hand. I still prefer the feel and heft of a book. (Heck, I even like the way a book smells!) The whispered crackle of spine and pages when I open a first edition of *David Copperfield* is just brilliant. I posit that you and your students will as well.

On-demand companies such as CreateSpace offer short runs (the number of books you plan to print), and they can even turn your student publications into ebooks (e.g., Kindle). One school I worked with ordered just enough books for the class. Another ordered several thousand and sold the books as a PTA fund-raiser. These companies typically offer very fast turnarounds and user-friendly tools. It can be as easy as snapping your fingers to the tune of Henry Mancini's "The Pink Panther." Don't believe me? Try it!

By this point, you should have your title, the entire completed manuscript, and the final cover design (or at least a strong concept). So, let's do it!

KwameTime
Video for Students
Setting Up A Classroom Publishing Company
(See page 19.)

Celebrating Your Published Authors

On the exciting day when the books come back from the printer, your students will officially be published. As Lucy Calkins says, "That matters because it inducts students into the writerly life. This has proven to lead to greater confidence in learning and academic success. Because publication can provide such focus and tap such energy, this must be one of the first priorities in the literate classroom."

Applaud your student authors who not only wrote publishable poems, but owned the publishing process. Relish in the fact that you have just changed many students' understanding of the word *possibility*.

The student's name was Adam. He was dressed in goth/emo attire, didn't talk through most of the writing exercises, wrote some very heavy poetry filled with the blues, and had very few friends. A teacher warned me that he was withdrawn. The day the books arrived at the school, I met each of the students in the library and passed out books. Adam came alive in a way that the teacher and I had never witnessed. He came up and hugged me and couldn't stop sharing his joy and enthusiasm. "Mr. Kwame, I'm going to write another book."

Giving Students Voice

Inevitably, publishing a book is an extraordinary and intensely gratifying accomplishment (I've done it 26 times, and it still feels just as exciting), but why it matters, why it's so integral and important in the writing workshop is because writers want to be read, which inspires them to write more—and that's the express purpose of *The Write Thing*: to give students voice and to build confidence.

QUESTIONS for KWAME

Have you always wanted to write, or did you find your passion later?
I didn't find my passion until college when I started writing social protest poetry (poetry to make my fellow students aware of all the social injustices on our campus and in our world) and love poems (poetry to let girls know I thought they were pretty special).

Solo Act: Kim Hardwick
Principal, Clayton Huey Elementary School in New York

While it is difficult to capture the magic that the writing workshop creates, I can tell you that the book launch party is one of the best moments I have been blessed enough to be a part of. This is when the students, now published poets, become rock stars. With friends and family members in attendance, a poetry reading often accompanies the book release. The students present their poems from the book and beam with confidence and pride. I've had students— elementary, middle, and high school—tell me that they never thought of themselves as "writers" until Book-in-a-Day, and now that they had been published once, why not again and again? Writing workshop empowers students to find their voices and proudly put them in print. Forever. For all to read. By the way, did I mention that four of our Book-in-a-Day students attended the Book Expo of America Convention at the Jacob Javits Center in New York City to autograph copies for the teachers, booksellers, and librarians from across the country? I told you, absolute rock stars!

YoU CAN Too!

1. Based on your classroom needs, how much time will you spend publishing your students' work?

2. Which part of the process do you think will be most difficult? How can you get extra support to make it successful?

3. Place your current students into the five production teams and think about how you can encourage your students to lead the publication of their work.

Part 3: Presenting

"The world we live in today requires students to effectively present their ideas with clarity, purpose, passion, persuasion, and confidence ... "
—Pooja Patel, Poet

"WE WORK HARD TO IMPROVE EVERY CHILD'S ABILITY TO READ AND TO WRITE. WE MUST COMMIT TO WORKING EQUALLY HARD... TO CREATE AN ENGAGING PRESENTATION, AND TO SPEAK WELL IN ALL SITUATIONS. THESE ARE CRUCIAL SKILLS."
—ERIC PALMER, POET

CHAPTER EIGHT

Presenting Student Work

At the end of my friend, Vinx's (the drummer who opened up for Sting) sets, he often brings up audience members, those who can sing (and even some who can't) to jam with him on stage. He's always very welcoming and nurturing, and inevitably, what results is musical magic, an experience full of wonder, serving up a thrilling surprise performance and a big boost of confidence to the chosen one. The same kind of magic can happen in writing workshop when students are given the opportunity to present their work. Classroom open mics, poetry slams, and poetry cafés are not only popular and positive activities for learning the art and appreciation of presentation and performance, but they also build effective communication skills with real-world applications.

The Joy of Presenting!

Now that your students have successfully published their work, it is time to present it to the public, sure to be one of the richest experiences of their writerly lives. The performance can happen in the classroom or in front of hundreds of students and parents at a formal school program. One teacher I know likes to set out candles on her table, dim the lights, and hold a monthly open mic that students eagerly look forward to. Another librarian hosts an after-school poetry reading with a jazz band comprised of students from the school band.

KwameTime Video for Teachers
Presenting Tips and Techniques
(See page 19.)

121

Fire Up Your Presentations

Whatever the venue and format, there is tremendous joy and enlightenment obtained in presenting original work in front of an audience. It's an awe-inspiring rush that I've experienced over the years, presenting around the world. I've gathered a few tips and techniques that you and your students may find useful. Here are four actions that you and your students can take to energize and invigorate your classroom and school presentations.

Invite Audience Participation

While performing poetry at Georgetown University in Washington, DC, I asked if anyone in the audience could beatbox. A young woman joined me on stage, began scatting and I had not only to keep pace and rhythm with her, but I had to modulate my voice so it all sounded cohesive. The synergy we created together was pure excitement and made for a dynamic performance! The audience even joined in clapping their hands and bopping their heads, and I knew then that I would make *Audience Interaction* a part of all my presentations.

Be Your True Self

During a book signing on my first book tour in Los Angeles, California, I took a creative risk and performed a gutsy love poem. In the pulpit of a church. I received a standing ovation, sold hundreds of books, and realized how important authenticity is in presenting and performance. Be your true self!

KwameTime Video for Students
Presenting 101: Tips for Success
(See page 19.)

Integrate Music, Song, and Multimedia

After attending a three-week writing fellowship in Tuscany, a friend of mine and I decided to travel to Paris for the weekend. We ventured to a jazz club, got introduced to the band, and before you know it, we were being asked to come up on stage and perform with the band. The performance was complete improvisation, which the audience enjoyed, and I was reminded of the power of collaboration and how exciting and entertaining it can be to integrate music, song, and multimedia into presentations.

Use Dramatic Interpretation and Props

At the American School in Singapore, a seventh grade student acted out the poem "Dribbling" from my novel *The Crossover*. He mesmerized the students, using movement,

Solo Act: Van G. Garrett
Poet and Middle School English Teacher

On our last night in the City of Lights, Kwame and I stumbled upon Le 9 Jazz Club. We entered the club, heavy backpacks and sports coats in hand, American tourists with ears tuned to jazz. I had already spent more money than I had, but the experience kept getting better and better and Kwame kept making me feel as if I could be the next great poet/artist in a place known for producing some of the greatest poets and artists.

We sat down and listened to the smooth sounds of Sylvia Howard, a beautiful woman who smiled at us from the moment that we came in. She knew that we were from elsewhere. She also knew how to sing in a way that felt like cotton candy to my ears—soft, unexpected, sugary. Some places just feel right. Some people know how to make you feel at home. Kwame had made me feel like family the whole time that I was in Europe. Sylvia made me feel comfortable from the first notes and pleasantries that she shared. Then came "Summertime."

I've heard many arrangements of "Summertime" over the years. However, I had never heard an arrangement so sexy that it made me hum, sing, and stomp my feet with such verve. Kwame also felt it. Snapped his fingers. Saw that I wanted to be a part of the action.

"Dude, you should get on the stage," he said. Caught up in the moment—I agreed. Just talking, not really thinking the opportunity would even present itself. It did. Sylvia came to our table during a break in sets. She found out that we were poets from the States, liked some of the same things—and the next thing I know I'm on stage, her bassist backing me up.

I had written about jazz in my book, Songs in Blue Negritude. *I'm also a musician (drummer). It seemed only fitting that I would be in a jazz club in Paris. However, getting on stage was not anything that I had "planned." But I knew I couldn't pass on the chance to perform my work. I wasn't concerned about "messing up." I teach my students not to worry about messing up—that sometimes in the mistake you can uncover something pretty remarkable; that what is most important is that you share your voice with the world. And that's how I felt in the moment. So, I grabbed my opportunity. It was impromptu. It was poetry. It was jazz. It was one of the highlights of my writing career.*

123

PARIS: LE 9 PERFORMANCE WITH SYLVIA HOWARD (SUMMER 2010)

we walked like leopards
jackets and bags

toward the back
couching weight smelling of jazz

as sylvia franc and peter
woodshed standards at le 9

bookending kwame and me
discussing art between sets

the hummingbird bespeaking
needed chills when performing

scaling stories of cars
female jazz singers

families and times
that colorizes music—

downbeats later i read
poems on her stage in paris

fingers snapping while succinct
bass walked to my lines

a requested encore—
a trio of poems

instruments sustaining full notes
deemed worthy of hugs and handshakes

i tucked them away like an emerald
gift wrapped in a sturdy brown bag

shining
all the way home

—*Van G. Garrett*

gestures, and facial expressions, as he embodied the poem without saying a word. In Konko Village, in the eastern region of Ghana, during a school presentation, I performed my first children's book *Acoustic Rooster and His Barnyard Band* for 200 elementary school kids, and wouldn't you know, during the performance, a black rooster walked over to me! What I learned from both of these experiences is that dramatic interpretation and props (even live ones) can make for a brilliant and memorable presentation.

The Basics of Presenting Powerfully

I always knew there was an art to presenting, but I didn't know, until very recently, that there is a scientific method. I was the Sunday keynote at a conference of aspiring children's book writers, which meant that I would have to listen to six other speakers dole out amazing advice and guidance on Friday and Saturday, and then totally rewrite my speech on Saturday night because everything I'd planned on saying had already been touched on. This is, in fact, exactly what happened.

As it happens, at a reception the night before my speech, I met a professor of speech communication near the bar (I was getting a glass of pineapple juice ...), and we struck up a conversation about public speaking and some of the

Solo Act: Toni Blackman
Poet, U.S. Department of State Hip Hop Ambassador

I've been working with youth and performance poetry since I was in high school, so I have many stories and hundreds of examples that illustrate the ways that poetry can change lives and inspire transformation. Every year for nine years I worked with a program called Sisters of the Circle. It was created to serve the immigrant refugees population in Roanoke and provide self-esteem development for teen girls through the arts. There were American girls from Virginia in this group along with girls from Haiti, Liberia, Sierra Leone, Tanzania, Somalia, Honduras, Dominican Republic, and Nepal. The group met weekly at the arts center and were provided snacks.

Some of the girls were just learning English and there was one girl who would not speak at all. Faraji was from Tanzania. She participated in the dance program some of the time and would write a few words but she would never speak. I would travel from New York to work at the Jefferson Center twice a year, and for almost three years all I could get from Faraji was a smile and a quiet hello. One day we were rehearsing for our big performance in the rehearsal hall and I was directing the girls onstage. The girls had a lot of after-school nervous energy and were not listening.

I was feeling frustrated so we took a juice break. When we gathered after the break, I started the girls out in a circle and did one of my cypher exercises with them. I then started assigning the pieces the girls had written. Because of English limitations, sometimes we would split one poem up amongst three girls, but I always supported and encouraged speaking even if it was only one word or one line. Sometimes it meant having choral delivery with two or three reciting together. I handed out the poems to everyone including Faraji.

I read the first two lines then called on Faraji to go next. I expected her normal giggle, eye roll, and head turn gesture but she recited two whole lines of poetry. She struggled with a few words and the other girls helped her. Their eyes opened wide and their faces lit up. One of the girls put her hand over her face in shock and another said out loud, "Miss Toni, you gon' act like that didn't just happened." I smiled and kept leading. The girls were opening for me at my concert and two days later we were doing a sound check. When it came time for Faraji to come onstage I wasn't sure she would do it, but when she said her two lines all of the girls stood up screaming to give her a standing ovation. Her breakthrough provided joy for the entire group and that next year when I came for my residency I had to ask her to be quiet a few times. It was the first time that having to discipline a student made me smile.

rhetorical devices that great speakers like Dr. Martin Luther King Jr. and John F. Kennedy used in their speeches. I thanked her for the enlightening conversation (I'd decided midway through my "pineapple" juice to focus my speech on inspiration, rather than information), she offered to critique my speech the next day and give me some feedback, and I went to my hotel room and wrote the speech.

The next day, I delivered a speech based on the "Basketball Rules" for life that are featured in *The Crossover*, only I used them as a metaphor for the writerly life. After the standing ovation, the professor of speech communication came up to me smiling profusely. I asked her how I did, and she gave me her notes, which consisted of a list of the rhetorical devices that I employed during the speech:

- **anaphora**—The repetition of a clause or phrase at the beginning of successive sentences
- **asyndeton**—The omission of conjunctions between words, sentences, clauses, in an effort to create emphasis
- **distinctio**—The specific/explicit reference to remove ambiguity
- **epizeuxis**—The repetition of one word for emphasis
- **humor**—Humor can be quite effective if used appropriately. Determine if humor is relevant to the topic and appropriate for the particular audience.
- **metaphor**—The comparison of one thing to another without the use of *like* or *as*
- **timing**—The timing of your presentation is critical. You don't want to ramble or rush—timing is best determined and controlled by lots of practice before the actual presentation.

Now, I may not have known that I was utilizing all these devices, but now that I do, I believe that my presentations can be even more powerful and enjoyable. The same applies for your students. By exposing your students to these and other rhetorical devices, they can develop a technique of using language effectively and persuasively in their presentations. This is an art, but it's also a science that employs various methods to convince, influence, and hopefully please an audience.

Bring Writing to Life: Methods for Presenting Poetry

The goal of the student presenter is to bring the material to life, to allow the listener to connect with the feelings conveyed in the piece, and to honor the words on the page as if they meant something to us all (because, they should). In order to accomplish this, students should understand the different methods of presenting their poems.

Reading

Reading from your paper, device, or book requires ample practice so that you can learn the best pacing for the poem—slow or fast—pronunciation, and rhythms of the poem. While it is not necessary to memorize every word, it's always a good thing to learn enough of it so that you can look up every now and then and see/connect with your audience. Once you gain significant confidence, experiment with the delivery and vocal variety. For example, what happens if you stress this word rather than that word?

Recitation

Reciting your poem requires the same preparation as reading, only you must memorize your poem. If you don't have the poem memorized, you're more likely to make mistakes when reciting it, even if you have it written down.

Kwame QuickTip

It's a great idea to let students listen to and watch poetry presentations and performances. A few of my favorites are HBO's *Brave New Voices*; readings by Maya Angelou, Billy Collins, Nikki Giovanni, and Naomi Shihab Nye; or any online video of a kid reciting Shel Silverstein's "Sick!"

Students should pay attention to what it is they like about the performances, notice the differences between *reading* and *recitation*, and become observers of the art of presentation. Use these questions to discuss the performances:

- What did you see, hear, and feel? What about the voice? What about their faces? Did you notice any distinct movements or gestures?

- What about the pace of their speech? Was it slow? Fast?

- Did you notice rhythm? Were they speaking in a certain rhythm or was it like regular conversation?

Lesson in Action

Learning to Present

It's So Emotional

Emotions are to poetry as improvisation is to jazz. It's a key element. Without it, you don't have the thing. We can feel emotions from reading words on the written page but sharing them when we recite a poem means using our voice, body language, and gestures along with our facial expressions. Here are a few dramatic exercises to help your students explore emotions:

- Have students each look into a mirror while you instruct them on which emotion to display. The mirror work is also a great self-acceptance exercise where students are asked to look into their own eyes.

- Place students in two lines facing one another. Give Line 1 an emotion to express, and ask the students in Line 2 to watch them while remaining as poker-faced as possible. Then Line 2 acts out an emotion while Line 1 observes.

- In pairs or teams of three or four, have students take turns reading in different character voices. How would a teacher recite this? How would a preacher deliver it? What about the president of the United States? Someone who is bored or doesn't care? A football coach? A young child? A mean or angry person? Someone who is very happy and excited?

Gestures are also important. The teacher can touch upon and give examples of locked body positions (e.g., hands behind one's back or in front, arms folded or hugging the body). It's also important to point out that some gestures can be distracting such as scratching and constantly fixing clothes.

Voice Play

Distribute a short poem to students. (My nine-year-old loves to recite Gwendolyn Brooks's "We Real Cool" in umpteen different voices, especially at bedtime.) Have the group brainstorm all the different ways the performer might play with the voice while reciting the poem. This is a great time to talk about and define rate of speech, rhythm, pitch, tone, and volume. Have students take turns reading the poem fast, then have someone read it slower and someone else even slower. Ask a student to read as if they were sharing in a noisy room, then in a quiet room or a library.

Plant Your Feet

Have students stand up and ask them to plant their feet. Lead a brief, guided visualization exercise where they see themselves like a plant with roots in the ground.

> *Stand up. Place your hand on your chair if you need to for balance. Close your eyes and take a deep breath from your belly. Breathe again, breathing in and out slowly. Let go of any tension in your shoulders or your neck. Move your head slowly from side to side and then bring it back to the center. With your eyes still closed, see yourself with your feet planted firmly on the ground. Imagine you are a tree with roots coming up from the earth. See yourself as strong, confident and ready to share your voice with the world. Take another breath, slowly open your eyes, then sit down.*

During presentations, invite students to evaluate how they did using the *Presenting Checklist: Student Self-Evaluation* (page 143). This checklist offers students an opportunity to think about the elements of good presentations and to reflect on how well they presented their work.

Hopefully no students fell asleep. Ask them whether it was easy or challenging to visualize themselves. Then, demonstrate a few examples of how not planting your feet can be distracting to an audience—feet shuffling, nervously tapping, or swaying.

I've written 26 books, and I still know most of the poems I wrote decades ago because I've read them so many times. The best way for students to memorize a poem is to read it out loud as many times as possible.

Here's a trick that works for me, when I'm trying to memorize a new poem:

1. Read your poem out loud.
2. Recite as much of the poem as you can, from the beginning, without looking at it.
3. Repeat these steps until you can recite the entire poem from memory.

Performance

Performing a poem can mean incorporating dramatic presentation, integrating voice, vocal changes, possibly song, and sometimes call and response. Use the acronym VOICE to help your students visualize an effective performance.

VOICE Acronym

V	O	I	C	E
Visualize	Outside/ Inside Voice	Interpret	Clarity	Energy
Vocalize	Open/Close	Instinctiveness	Consciousness	Excitement

Visualize your words. Vocalize (project) so others can hear you.

Outside/inside voices can create dramatic effects. Open/close performances with style (bring your individuality to the stage).

Interpret your work in meaningful ways. Instinctiveness is the key to dynamic work.

Clarity allows others to hear your hard work. Consciousness means that you are in sync with your audience.

Energy means giving the audience your best. Excitement means giving and receiving to and from the audience.

Harness Your Inner Greatness

Bringing all these elements of presentation together allows students to harness the greatness inside them. This process can create an innovative and holistic literacy lab in the classroom that allows students to explore, expand, and exercise their artistic muscles while giving them powerful tools to write, read, memorize, and recite their work. The repetition of these efforts helps lessen fear of judgment and feelings of awkwardness and creates a vibrant community of poetry giants in your school.

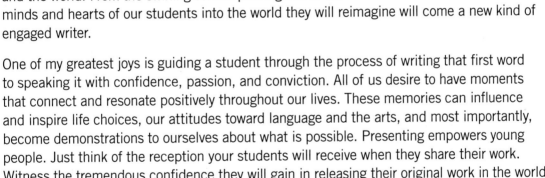

KwameTime
Video for Teachers
Kwame's Top 10
The Write Thing *Tips*
(See page 19.)

Just think, from elementary to secondary classrooms, students will take these rich experiences with them into their homes, schools, future colleges, universities, careers, and the world. From the swirling stories pouring out of the minds and hearts of our students into the world they will reimagine will come a new kind of engaged writer.

One of my greatest joys is guiding a student through the process of writing that first word to speaking it with confidence, passion, and conviction. All of us desire to have moments that connect and resonate positively throughout our lives. These memories can influence and inspire life choices, our attitudes toward language and the arts, and most importantly, become demonstrations to ourselves about what is possible. Presenting empowers young people. Just think of the reception your students will receive when they share their work. Witness the tremendous confidence they will gain in releasing their original work in the world through spoken word and presentation.

YOU CAN Too!

1. Which rhetorical devices do you regularly use in your teaching?

2. How can you teach students the differences among reading, reciting, and performing? Why is that important?

3. What else do you focus on with students when helping them improve their presentation skills?

Appendixes

"If you have access to a good library and a steady stream of student writing, you've got the most important resources you'll need."
—JoAnn Portalupi and Ralph Fletcher

"NOT ONLY DID YOU HELP US STUDENTS PUBLISH A BOOK TO BE PROUD OF, BUT **YOU HELPED US REALIZE OUR POTENTIAL TO DO ANYTHING WHEN WE SAY YES."**
—LAUREN, STUDENT AT LOUDOUN COUNTY HIGH SCHOOL, LEESBURG, VIRGINIA

Table of Contents

Name: _____ Date:_____

Imagery Chart

Directions: Imagery means that you're using figurative language in ways that appeal to the senses (sight, sound, touch, smell, and taste). To develop your understanding of figurative language and imagery, watch for it in your independent reading. In the left column, write the imagery language you spot. In the right column, classify it.

Imagery Language   **Classification**

_____   _____

_____   _____

_____   _____

_____   _____

_____   _____

_____   _____

_____   _____

Classification

- **Figurative language** includes similes, metaphors, personification, alliteration, hyperbole, and onomatopoeia.

- **Sensory details** help bring writing to life and draw readers into the text. Adding sensory details (e.g., the hook-billed, slate grey vulture) helps readers experience the writing as though they were there. Adjectives help set mood and tone in the text and help establish a strong voice.

- **Action verbs** crackle and pop; bristle with energy and swing with action.

(imagerychart.pdf; imagerychartprimary.pdf)

Annotated List of Poetry Forms

acrostic: poetry in which certain letters, usually the first in each line, form a word or message when read in a sequence

ballad: a poem that tells a story similar to a folktale or legend that often has a repeated refrain

bio: a poem written about one's life, personality traits, and ambitions

blackout: poetry created by covering up most of a page of text (from a book, magazine article, etc.) while leaving key, specially chosen words that make a poem

blank verse: a poem written in unrhymed iambic pentameter; The iambic pentameter form often resembles the rhythms of speech.

borrowed: poetry that uses words or lines from other poems to create a new poem

burlesque: poetry that treats a serious subject as humor

canzone: Medieval Italian lyric style poetry with five or six stanzas and a shorter ending stanza

carpe diem: Latin expression that means "seize the day;" *carpe diem* poems have a theme of living for today.

cinquain: a short poem of five, usually unrhymed lines containing, respectively, two, four, six, eight, and two syllables; Line 1 has one word (the title). Line 2 has two words that describe the title. Line 3 has three words that tell the action. Line 4 has four words that express the feeling. Line 5 has one word that recalls the title.

classicism: poetry that holds the principles and ideals of beauty that are characteristic of Greek and Roman art, architecture, and literature

clerihew: a four-line verse—and the namesake of Edmund Clerihew Bentley, who was born in 1875 and crafted the first clerihew comprising:

- rhyming couplets of AA, BB
- a person's name as its first line
- something to say about that person
- and it should make you smile

concrete: poetry written in the shape or form of an object; also known as a shape poem

couplet: rhyming stanzas made up of two lines

Annotated List of Poetry Forms (cont.)

diamond or diamante: a diamond-shaped poem with seven lines that describes a particular topic by using one noun on the first and seventh lines, two adjectives on the second and sixth lines, three action verbs in the third and fifth lines, and four nouns in the fourth line; It can also be used to describe two contrasting subjects.

dramatic monologue: a type of poem that is spoken to a listener; The speaker addresses a specific topic while the listener unwittingly reveals details about themselves. (also known as a persona poem)

elegy: a sad and thoughtful poem about the death of an individual

epic: an extensive, serious poem that tells the story of a heroic figure

epigram: a very short, ironic, witty poem usually written as a brief couplet or quatrain; The term is derived from the Greek word *epigramma*, meaning *inscription*.

epitaph: a commemorative inscription on a tomb or mortuary monument written to praise the deceased

epithalamium (*epithalamion*): a poem written in honor of a bride and groom

free verse (*vers libre*): a poem written in either rhyme or unrhymed lines that has no set fixed metrical pattern

ghazal: a short lyrical poem that arose in Urdu; It is between 5 and 15 couplets long. Each couplet contains its own poetic thought but is linked in rhyme that is established in the first couplet and continued in the second line of each pair. The lines of each couplet are equal in length. Themes are usually connected to love and romance. The closing signature often includes the poet's name or an allusion to it.

haiku: a Japanese poem composed of three unrhymed lines of five, seven, and five syllables, usually containing a season word

Horatian ode: short lyric poem written in two- or four-line stanzas, each with the same metrical pattern, often addressed to a friend, which deals with friendship, love, and the practice of poetry; It is named after its creator, Horace.

iambic pentameter: one short syllable followed by one long one, five sets in a row (da-DAH da-DAH da-DAH da-DAH da-DAH)

Annotated List of Poetry Forms (cont.)

idyll: poetry that either depicts a peaceful, idealized country scene or a long poem telling a story about heroes of a bygone age

irregular (pseudo-Pindaric or Cowleyan) **ode**: neither the three-part form of the Pindaric ode nor the two- or four-line stanza of the Horatian ode; It is characterized by irregularity of verse and structure and lack of correspondence between the parts.

Italian sonnet: a sonnet consisting of an octave with the rhyme pattern ABBAABBA followed by six lines with a rhyme pattern of CDECDE or CDCDCD

lay: a long narrative poem, especially one that was sung by Medieval minstrels

limerick: a short, sometimes vulgar, humorous poem consisting of five anapestic lines; Lines 1, 2, and 5 have seven to ten syllables, rhyme, and have the same verbal rhythm. Lines 3 and 4 have five to seven syllables, rhyme, and have the same rhythm.

list: a poem that is made up of a list; It can be any length and rhymed or unrhymed.

lyric: a poem that expresses the thoughts and feelings of the poet

memoriam stanza: a quatrain in iambic tetrameter with a rhyme scheme of ABBA—named after the pattern used by Lord Tennyson

name: poetry that tells about a word; It uses the letters of a word as the first letter of each line.

narrative: a poem that tells a story

ode: a lengthy lyric poem, typically of a serious or meditative nature, that has an elevated style and formal stanza structure

pastoral: a poem that depicts rural life in a peaceful, romanticized way

Petrarchan: a 14-line sonnet consisting of an octave rhyming ABBAABBA followed by a sestet of CDDCEE or CDECDE

Pindaric ode: a ceremonious poem consisting of a strophe (two or more lines repeated as a unit) followed by an antistrophe with the same metrical pattern and concluding with a summary line (an epode) in a different meter; named after Pindar, a Greek professional lyricist of the fifth century BC

Annotated List of Poetry Forms (cont.)

quatrain: a stanza or poem consisting of four lines; Lines 2 and 4 must rhyme while having a similar number of syllables.

rhyme: a rhyming poem has the repetition of the same or similar sounds of two or more words, often at the end of the line

rhyme royal: a type of poetry consisting of stanzas having seven lines in iambic pentameter

romanticism: a poetic movement about nature and love while having emphasis on the personal experience

rondeau: a lyrical poem of French origin having 10 or 13 lines with two rhymes and with the opening phrase repeated twice as the refrain

senryu: a short Japanese-style poem, similar to haiku in structure, that treats human beings rather than nature, often in a humorous or satiric way

sestina: a poem consisting of six six-line stanzas and a three-line envoy; The end words of the first stanza are repeated in varied order as end words in the other stanzas and also recur in the envoy.

Shakespearean: a 14-line sonnet consisting of three quatrains of ABAB CDCD EFEF followed by a couplet, GG; Shakespearean sonnets generally use iambic pentameter.

shape: poetry written in the shape or form of an object

sonnet: a lyric poem that consists of 14 lines which usually have one or more conventional rhyme schemes

tanka: a Japanese poem of five lines, the first and third composed of five syllables each and the other lines have seven syllables each

Terza rima: a type of poetry consisting of 10- or 11-syllable lines arranged in three-line tercets

verse: a single, metrical line of poetry

villanelle: a 19-line poem consisting of five tercets and a final quatrain on two rhymes; The first and third lines of the first tercet repeat alternately as a refrain closing the succeeding stanzas and joined as the final couplet of the quatrain.

(annotatedlist.pdf)

Kwame's Ingredients of Poetry

Ingredients of Poetry

Serving Size: Unlimited
Servings per Day: Unlimited

	% Daily Value*
Brevity	100%
Conciseness	100%
Feeling	100%
Figurative Language	100%
Form	100%
Imagination	100%
Originality	100%
Passion	100%
Repetition	100%
Rhyme	100%
Rhythm	100%

*Percent Daily Values are based on a 6-hour school day.

(ingredientsposter.pdf)

Name: _____ **Date:** _____

Does This Poem Have the Right Ingredients?

Kwame Alexander's Definition of Poetry

Poetry is an original arrangement of words in a concise manner that uses rhythm, form, and figurative language to express a meaningful thought or experience. It creates an emotional response by showing something significant rather than telling it.

Title of poem: _____

- ❏ Is the poem authentic? Is it sharing a truth?
- ❏ Is the poet using the best form to convey the idea? (e.g., Would the poem have been better unrhymed?)
- ❏ Did the poet use the right words? Is the diction spot on?
- ❏ Are there unnecessary small words (e.g., and, a, an, of) and punctuation?
- ❏ Does the poem contain clear and concrete images?
- ❏ Does the poem evoke and show, not tell?
- ❏ Will the reader have a strong emotional (or intellectual) reaction that makes them feel or think something significant?

(ingredients.pdf; ingredientsprimary.pdf)

Name: _____ Date:_____

Presenting Checklist: Student Self-Evaluation

Always speak with confidence, passion, and conviction.—Kwame Alexander

Presentation Title

_____

Elements	Considerations	Reflection
Voice	• Speaks with a clear, confident voice • Enunciates clearly • Stresses key words for dramatic or humorous affect • Demonstrates strong vocal control, changing voice as needed to emphasize emotions of the piece • Emphasizes rhythm of piece • Pacing is just right; not too fast or slow	
Body	• Plants feet and stands straight and tall • Relaxed and confident demeanor reflected in strong, steady stance • Manages hands gracefully (behind back, folded in front, at sides) • Aligns gestures with voice to add emphasis • Uses gestures to dramatic effect	
Face	• Makes eye contact with the audience • Relaxed confidence reflected on face; conveys "true self" • Smiles when appropriate	
Presentation	• Incorporates music, dramatic interpretation, movement, or props into presentation • Demonstrates confidence, passion, and conviction	

(presentingchecklist.pdf)

5W Poems

Overview

A 5W poem draws from the conventions of a news story by asking who, what, where, when, and why. This format can produce short poems, as well as help students develop their comprehension and summarization skills.

> Langston Hughes
> wrote the "Negro Speaks of Rivers"
> on a train to Mexico
> when he was 18 years old
> to celebrate the strength of the black community.

Lesson

1. Read different 5W poems and ask students to describe the characteristics. Record the observations on a chart.

2. Show the students the format of a 5W poem and explain that the 5Ws are used in journalism to highlight and summarize the key points of a news story. This format also can be used to generate non-rhyming poems.

Line 1: Who	
Line 2: What	
Line 3: Where	
Line 4: When	
Line 5: Why	

3. Using a website such as **biography.com**, **poetryfoundation.org**, or **poets.org**, write a shared poem about a famous writer. Record notes that answer the questions who, what, where, when, and why.

4. Once the shared poem is completed, ask students to pick topics and write their own 5W poems. Students can write about famous figures, but they may also look through newspaper stories and use the details to craft poems.

5. Ask the students to polish their poems and share them with the class.

Cinquain Poems

Overview

Cinquain poems are five-line poems with 22 syllables (2, 4, 6, 8, and 2):

Line 1: Two syllables
Line 2: Four syllables
Line 3: Six syllables
Line 4: Eight syllables
Line 5: Two syllables

Homework
takes much too long
it snatches your free time
and rattles your brain until you
give up!

Peanut
butter jelly
sandwiches for breakfast
make me hyperactive all day—
then CRASH!

Lesson

1. Use a mind map to create a scene. Write the scene in the middle and record impressions and details in the spokes.

2. Write a draft of a cinquain on a sheet of paper using the mind map for ideas.

3. Describe the central scene using the right number of syllables for each line.

4. Arrange and revise the poem using the rules for a cinquain poem and highlight the central image.

5. Underline your favorite words and phrases.

6. Publish a final draft according to the rules of this form.

Alternate Format Cinquain

Title (optional)
Line 1: One word
Line 2: Two words
Line 3: Three words
Line 4: Four words
Line 5: One word

Golden
First
sign of
daylight, yellow flower
parts lips for morning
kiss.

Cinquain poems by Chris Colderley

145

Color Poems

Overview

Playing with colors and the five senses offers students an easy entry into poetry and an exciting new world of figurative language such as metaphor, simile, and personification.

Resources

- "Color" by Christina Rossetti
- copies of *Color Poems Chart* (colorpoems.pdf)

Lesson

1. Read aloud "Color" by Christina Rossetti, and identify the way she describes different colors in her poem.

2. Ask students to each pick a color and describe it for someone else.

3. Ask students to expand their descriptions by adding details and images. For example, students might say *yellow is the sun*. Encourage them to build this comparison by adding details such as *yellow is the sound of splashing water* or *yellow is melting ice cream*.

4. Allow students time to identify different sounds, smells, tastes, and textures to describe a color and complete the chart.

5. When students have completed the chart, ask them to select the most interesting comparisons to draft color poems. Allow time for students to compose color poems that include similes, metaphors, and imagery.

Extension

Have students make collages that complement the messages in their poems.

APPENDIX B / POETRY FORM MINI LESSONS / COLOR POEMS CHART

Sense	Description
How does the color smell?	
What does the color feel like?	
What does the color look like?	
What does the color sound like?	
What does the color taste like?	
What kind of feelings are this color?	
What places and experiences are this color?	

I Am From Poems

Overview

Students will use memories to craft poems about the places they come from. The poem "Where I'm From" by George Ella Lyon is a collection of memories from the author's past. The text recollects important times, places, and people from the author's past by drawing on all five senses.

Resources

- "Where I'm From" by George Ella Lyon
- copies of *Where I'm From Chart* (iamfrom.pdf)

Lesson

1. Read "Where I'm From" by George Ella Lyon to students.

2. To create your own example "Where I'm From" poem, begin brainstorming things from your past. Use the *Where I'm From Chart* to guide your discussion.

3. Select the most interesting phrases and organize them into a draft using modeled writing and think alouds.

4. Arrange the phrases to highlight a central image. Consider adding some poetic techniques such as onomatopoeia, simile, metaphor, or imagery.

5. Allow time for students to complete their own charts and write I Am From poems.

WHERE I'M FROM

I am from clothespins,
from Clorox and carbon-tetrachloride.
I am from the dirt under the back porch.
(Black, glistening
it tasted like beets.)
I am from the forsythia bush,
the Dutch elm
whose long-gone limbs I remember
As if they were my own.

I am from fudge and eyeglasses,
    from Imogene and Alafair.
I'm from the know-it-alls
    and the pass-it-ons,
from Perk up! and Pipe down!
I'm from He restoreth my soul
    with a cottonball lamb
    and ten verses I can say myself.

I'm from Artemus and Billie's Branch,
fried corn and strong coffee.
From the finger my grandfather lost
    to the auger,
the eye my father shut to keep his sight.

Under my bed was a dress box
spilling old pictures,
a sift of lost faces
to drift beneath my dreams.
I am from those moments—
snapped before I budded—
leaf-fall from the family tree.

—*George Ella Lyon*

I Am Pizzazz Poems

Overview

An I Am Pizzazz poem is a popular form that allows students to describe themselves using a set formula. Using Kwame Alexander's poem "Filthy McNasty," students will write an I Am Pizzazz poem that describes themselves in unique and interesting ways.

Resources

- Alexander, K. (2014). *The Crossover.* Houghton Mifflin Harcourt.

- copies of *I Am Pizzazz Chart* (iampizzazz.pdf)

Memories	Description
Details about the home and the neighborhood where you grew up	
Objects from your home and your neighborhood that you remember well	
Names of places that you still remember vividly	
Sayings and phrases that you used or heard	
Favorite foods	
Names of important people and relatives	

Lesson

1. Read aloud the poem "Filthy McNasty" by Kwame Alexander, and identify the different ways the speaker identifies himself.

2. Highlight the use of interesting language to create rhythm and add excitement.

   - ***–ing verbs***—elevating and agitating
   - **Alliteration**—dubious distinction
   - **Rhyme**—classy and sassy
   - **Gobblefunk (invented words)**—combinating, uncooled, and slamerific
   - **Talking about yourself in the 3rd person**—when Filthy gets hot

3. Ask each student to fill out the chart. Emphasize that this exercise is about brainstorming ideas.

4. Once students have completed brainstorming, encourage them to create interesting descriptions by using words in creative and interesting ways. For example, a "good speaker" could be changed to "silver-tongued talking."

5. When they have created several interesting phrases, encourage students to organize them into drafts that highlight central images.

6. Ask students to consider adding some techniques used in the mentor poem, such as –*ing* verbs, alliteration, gobblefunk, and rhyme to add pizzazz to the final versions.

I Love Poems

I LOVE THE NATIONAL PASTIME
I love baseball The crack of the bat The slap of the mitt And the umpire yelling, "Yer out!"

Overview

Eloise Greenfield's book, *Honey, I Love*, is written through the eyes of a child about things they love, such as riding a train and skipping rope. In this lesson, students re-examine their conception of love poems by investigating different kinds of love and finding joy in the events of everyday life.

Resource

Greenfield, E. (2016). *Honey, I Love, And Other Love Poems*. HarperCollins.

Lesson

1. Read *Honey, I Love* by Eloise Greenfield, and ask students to contribute to a shared list of things and people they love. Discuss which items are unique or unexpected.

2. Have students each draw a large heart on a blank sheet of paper. Ask them to write things they love in the centers of their hearts. For example, they could answer these questions on their papers:

   - What are your favorite activities?

   - What is your favorite meal?

   - Who is someone you greatly admire?

3. Have each student choose one item from the list they would like to write about.

4. Students should brainstorm words and phrases that explain what they love about their topics in more detail. If they choose a sport, they should add rich details:

   - Are there any special smells or tastes that you associate with this sport?

   - What equipment do you need to play the sport?

   - What sounds do you hear when you play this sport?

   - When do you think the sport is most exciting?

5. Ask students to use the mentor poem, "Honey, I Love," to organize their thoughts into lines and stanzas.

6. When they have drafts, students should revise them by adding poetic techniques such as simile, metaphor, and imagery, as well as rhyme.

I Remember Poems

Overview

Poets often get ideas for writing by listening to stories, recalling experiences, and brainstorming topics. In this lesson, we examine different poems to consider how poets get ideas for their writing. In the poem "Bedtime," Ralph Fletcher begins by remembering "the good old days."

Resource

"Bedtime" by Ralph Fletcher

Lesson

1. Ralph Fletcher used his memories of a special time and place to get the idea for his poem. Can you think of other poems that recall stories about the past?

2. Ask students to begin by thinking about a place that has special memories for them.

3. Have students draw sketches that show important details of these special places. Include labels and captions if they help crystallize the images. The sketches should remind students of special moments. For example, "This is the hook where my mother hung her apron after she finished the dishes."

4. Ask students to share their drawings and memories with partners and use these to begin lists of ideas for their poems.

5. Tell students to select the most interesting phrases and organize them into drafts.

6. Arrange the phrases to highlight central images. Have students consider adding some poetic techniques, such as onomatopoeia, simile, metaphor, and imagery, to add interest to the final versions.

BEDTIME

Sometimes I remember
the good old days

sitting on the kitchen floor
at night with my brother

each on our own squares
of cold linoleum.

I'm fresh from the bath,
wearing baseball pyjamas.

Outside the screen door
summer breezes stir.

Mom gives us each two cookies,
a cup of milk, a kiss good-night.

I still can't imagine anything
better than that.

—*Ralph Fletcher*

If You Find Poems

Overview

If You Find poems ask writers to give advice about what to do if you find a specific object. Writers may identify real items, such as a pencil, a baseball card, or apple. They also may choose imaginary items, such as rubber pens, Martian spaceships, or Batman's tool belt. The exercise can provide serious advice for the reader or it may attempt to be humorous.

Resource

MacKay, E. 2013. *If You Hold a Seed*. Running Press Kids.

Lesson

1. Read *If You Hold a Seed* by Elly MacKay to students.

2. With students, make a list of objects that you might find in the classroom, in your home, or on the street.

3. Model for students how to pick an object that you think is the most interesting to write about. Then, through modeled writing, make a list of all the real and imaginary things you could do with that object.

Example: A Book

- Act out the story.
- Jump on it like a trampoline.
- Make connections.
- Pretend it's your pet.
- Rip it apart.
- Use it as a shield.

IF YOU FIND A BOOK

Say, "Hello"
and shake its
hand
enjoy the stories
and spend the day
strolling
along the shore

wear it like a hat
when you act
out each part

when you are
finished
pretend it's your pet

take it for
an afternoon walk
fly it like a plane
ride it like a
skateboard
jump on it
like a trampoline
and throw it
like a Frisbee

save it like
a smile
for bad days

—*Chris Colderley*

If You Find Poems (cont.)

Example: A Book (cont.)

- Draw on it.
- Learn new things.
- Make it into papier mâché.
- Talk about it with your friends.
- Use it as a skateboard.
- Eat it for breakfast.
- Make it fly like a plane.
- Read it.
- Throw it like a Frisbee.
- Wear it like a hat.

4. Show students how to select the most interesting phrases and organize them into a draft.

5. Arrange the phrases to highlight a central image. Consider adding some poetic techniques, such as onomatopoeia, simile, metaphor, and imagery, to add interest to the final version.

6. Allow time for students to brainstorm and write their own poems.

Extension

Repeat the process after choosing an imaginary object, such as a genie's bottle, Superman's cape, or an invisibility cloak.

If You Poems

Overview

These poems allow you to use the senses to paint a powerful image.

Resource

"Lemon Tree" by Jennifer Clement

Lesson

1. Read the poem, "Lemon Tree" by Jennifer Clement. Complete the sensory organizer using this poem. (See example chart below.)

2. Model for students how to pick an item and describe the item through the five senses: sight, sound, smell, taste, and touch.

3. Work with students to pick a situation to describe in your poem.

LEMON TREE

If you climb a lemon tree
feel the bark
under your knees and feet,
smell the white flowers,
carve the leaves
between your hands.

Remember,
the tree is older than you are
and you might find stories
in its branches.

—Jennifer Clement

Sense	Description
Sight	lemon tree, white flowers
Sound	
Smell	lemons, white flowers
Taste	lemons
Touch	feel the bark under your knees and feet, carve the leaves between your hands.

If You Poems (cont.)

4. Select the most interesting phrases, and organize them into a draft, using a think aloud to model for students. Arrange the phrases to highlight a central image. Consider adding some poetic techniques, such as onomatopoeia, simile, metaphor, and imagery, to add interest to the final version.

5. Have students write their own If You poems. Suggest they begin their poems with any of the following phrases:

If you find . . .

- a hockey stick
- a bird's nest
- a basketball
- a squished blueberry
- a cow bell
- an old ball

- a cupcake hat
- a duck in your pool
- a marker
- a frog in your pond
- a red wig
- a butterfly net

GRILLED CHEESE

If you find a grilled cheese sandwich
Touch the warm bread with your
fingers
And feel the crispy crust
Watch gooey cheese
ooze
     out
         over
            the
               edges
Smell the buttery bread
Taste it all come together

— *Dylan, Grade 4*

THE ROOT BEER

if you find root beer
in your fridge
stop and open it,
watch and smell the fizz
drink it like a river
flowing through your mouth,
into your stomach,
then it's a lake
with fish jumping
up and down and
boats sailing around.

— *Connor, Grade 4*

Invitation Poems

Overview

Alice Schertle's poem, "Invitation from a Mole," takes the reader on a tour of a mole's underground home. The poem has lines of different lengths and uses some concrete elements to add a visual impact. For example, the line "on the tip of your tongue" sticks out a little bit from the rest of the text. It looks like a tongue sticking out.

Resources

- Schertle, A. & Minor, W. (1999). *A Lucky Thing*. HMH Books for Young Readers.
- Sidman, J. & Allen, R. (2014). *Winter Bees & Other Poems of the Cold*. HMH Books for Young Readers.

Lesson

1. Begin by reading "Invitation from a Mole" aloud and identifying the parts of the mole's home that are revealed.

2. After reading through the poem, ask students to identify sensory details from the text. Use a chart to record the different images.

Sense	Description
Sight	
Sound	
Smell	
Taste	
Touch	

3. Ask students to pick an animal and research its characteristics. Find out where it lives, what it eats, and what kind of activities it performs.

Invitation Poems (cont.)

4. When they have collected their notes, allow time for students to draft their own invitation poems.

5. Have students write poems inviting humans to visit. They should begin their poems by thinking about the animals' habitats. For animals that live underground, "Come on down …" If the animal lives in a tree, "Come on up …"

6. Remind students to add visual details to make their poems more interesting for readers.

Adapted from Pritchard, J. (2009). Module 3: Poetry Break—Poem That Does Not Rhyme. Pritchardspoetry.blogspot.ca from pritchardspoetry.blogspot.ca/2009/03/module-3-poetry-break-poem-that-does.html

---

INVITATION FROM A MOLE

come on down

live among worms awhile
taste dirt
      on the tip of your tongue

smell
      the sweet damp feet of mushrooms
listen to roots
         reaching
           deeper

press your cheek against
the cold face of a stone

wear the earth like a glove
close   your   eyes
wrap yourself in darkness

     see

what you're missing

      —*from* A Lucky Thing *by Alice Schertle*

Place Poems

Overview

Describing a place can be a difficult task. In the rush to be somewhere else, people often miss the unique details of their environment. Nikki Giovanni's poem, "Knoxville, Tennessee," recounts her memories of a place and time that was very special in her life.

Resource

"Knoxville, Tennessee" by Nikki Giovanni

Lesson

1. After reading through the poem, ask students to identify sensory details from the text. Use a chart to record the different images. (See the chart on page 155.)

2. Discuss how the sensory details in the poem show how the author feels about Knoxville.

3. Point out some of the unique qualities of the poem. Giovanni's use of short lines, as well as "and" throughout the poem, give the reader the sense that an excited child is retelling their story about a nonstop day in Knoxville.

4. Ask students to think about the places they live, as well as their favorite seasons. Brainstorm activities, foods, sounds, sights, and feelings they experience. Have students pick special places that have strong memories for them.

5. Have students use the names of their chosen places for the titles of their poems.

6. Allow time for students to write poems that begin, "I always like [SEASON] best." Encourage students to use as many sensory details as possible in their poems.

Preposition Poems

Overview

One poetry technique related to "The Red Wheelbarrow" by William Carlos Williams is composing preposition poems. A preposition is a word (or group of words) that indicates the relationship, often spatial, of one object to another. In preposition poems, students begin each line with a preposition. This form is a great way to help students develop their powers of observation and description. The result also can be very poetic and lyrical.

Lesson

1. Have each student or student groups begin by picking an object or an event.

2. Using phrases that start with prepositions, describe the object or event in relation to other things in as many ways as you can.

3. Revise the order of the phrases—chronologically, top to bottom, left to right, etc.— to highlight a central image.

Common One-Word Prepositions

aboard	besides	into	than
about	between	like	through
above	beyond	minus	to
across	but	near	toward
after	by	of	under
against	concerning	off	underneath
along	considering	on	unlike
amid	despite	onto	until
among	down	opposite	up
anti	during	outside	upon
around	except	over	versus
as	excepting	past	via
at	excluding	per	with
before	following	plus	within
behind	for	regarding	without
below	from	round	
beneath	in	save	
beside	inside	since	

Renga

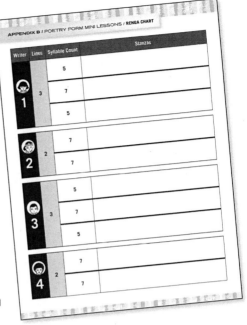

Overview

A renga is a collaborative poem of Japanese origin. The first writer begins with a haiku—three lines of seventeen syllables. The next writer adds two lines each with seven syllables. The third writer adds a haiku. The fourth writer adds two lines each with seven syllables. This pattern continues until the poem is complete. Each stanza should be able to stand on its own and should only advance from the preceding stanza.

Resources

- Alexander, K. (2014). *The Crossover.* Houghton Mifflin Harcourt. "Tanka for Language Arts Class" (212).

- Alexander, K. (2007). *Crush: Love Poems.* Word of Mouth Books.

- copies of *Renga Chart* (renga.pdf)

Lesson

1. Once students understand haiku (pages 78–79) and tanka (page 168) poems, they can try a renga.

2. Introduce the pattern:
   - The first writer begins with a haiku—three lines of seventeen syllables.
   - The next writer adds two lines each with seven syllables.
   - The third writer adds a haiku.
   - The fourth writer adds two lines each with seven syllables.
   - This pattern continues until the poem is complete.

3. Explain that renga often has a seasonal theme, like haiku, but it also can be humorous or funny.

Renga (cont.)

4.   Remind students that each stanza should be able to stand on its own and should only advance from the preceding stanza. In other words, they should pay attention to the previous stanza in their own writing.

5.   Give each student a sheet of paper, and ask them to write their name in the top right.

6.   Give them five minutes to compose original haiku.

7.   Then, ask them to pass their haiku to other students. Arrange the grouping so that each student only writes once on any sheet.

8.   Ask students to leave a blank line after the original haiku. Allow them three minutes to compose the next stanzas for the poems.

9.   Continue the process until each student has his or her own poem again. Initially, you might only pass a poem four or five times before returning it to the owner. As students gain confidence, you can increase the number of writers for each poem.

10.   Once the first writer has their copy back, they should compose the final stanza for the poem. The first writer should count the syllables in each line and make any corrections in spelling and grammar.

11.   Once the process is complete, students should publish the final copies. The class renga can then be put together in a collection.

Senryu

Overview

A senryu is described as a haiku with attitude. It is written in haiku form but has wit and insight instead of pure description. Senryu often include "observational" humor about human nature.

Resource

Muth, J. (2014). *Hi, Koo!: A year of seasons*. Scholastic.

Lesson

1. Model for students how to use the headings *Who*, *What*, and *Where* to record some observations about a scene.

2. Make a list of things that bother you, and then add some details.

3. Use the details to write a single sentence. Cross out words that do not help to create a clear image.

4. Write out the sentence in three lines like a haiku.

5. Count the syllables in each line (5, 7, 5).

6. Tinker with the syllables and word choice to make the senryu witty and insightful.

7. Publish your final copy.

So Much Depends Poems

Overview

"The Red Wheelbarrow" is a short four-stanza poem made up of only 17 words. The author, William Carlos Williams, was a family doctor in New Jersey who also wrote poetry. He wanted to write poetry that related to the everyday life of people and was written in plain, straightforward language. Most of the inspiration for his poems came directly from his own observations and experiences.

At first, most students are unimpressed by the work, and the boldest ones express reservations about whether this is really a poem. The genius of this poem is that it cuts to the heart of what poetry is really about—changing the way the reader (and the writer) sees the world. The effect of a good poem can be so powerful that the reader is permanently changed after the reading.

THE RED WHEELBARROW	THE WHITE CHALK
so much depends upon	so much depends upon
a red wheel barrow	a white piece of chalk
glazed with rain water	writing new knowledge
beside the white chickens.	on the classroom blackboard.
—*William Carlos Williams*	—*Chris Colderley*
	(inspired by William Carlos Williams)

So Much Depends Poems (cont.)

Resource

"The Red Wheelbarrow" by William Carlos Williams

Lesson

1. Using the example of "The Red Wheelbarrow," challenge students to write their own poems by looking around the classroom and brainstorming items—for example, writing depends on a pencil, reading depends on a book, and games depend on a ball.

2. Have students develop their images by observing and brainstorming what they see: What color is it? What does it do? What is the shape? Where is it located? Once they have recorded about 20 observations, they are ready to begin writing.

3. Tell each student to arrange their phrases in a pattern similar to the original poem.

4. Have students consider adding some poetic techniques, such as alliteration, onomatopoeia, and imagery, to add interest to the final versions.

Sports Poems: Onomatopoeia

Overview

The relationship between poetry and sports goes back to ancient Greece. Pindar, for example, wrote odes in honor of Olympic athletes. In modern times, poets have continued this tradition by celebrating the modern sports of baseball and basketball, to name a few. Sports are filled with many sights, sounds, smells, tastes, and textures, which make sports a great subject for writing rich poetry.

Resources

- Alexander, K. (2014). *The Crossover*. Houghton Mifflin Harcourt.
- "Analysis of Baseball" by May Swenson
- "Casey at the Bat" by Ernest Lawrence Thayer
- "Foul Shot" by Edwin A. Hoey
- "Slam, Dunk, & Hook" by Yusef Komunyakaa

Lesson

1. Begin by reading "Dribbling" by Kwame Alexander.
2. Ask students to identify some of the features that make this poem unique.
    - Alexander uses visual elements to mimic some of the movements from basketball.
    - Alexander repeats the –*ing* sound throughout the poem to create rhythm, much like a bouncing ball.
    - Alexander uses onomatopoeia—words that imitate the sounds they describe—to recreate the atmosphere of basketball.
3. Make a list of words from sports that imitate the sounds they are describing.
4. Have students pick their favorite sports and identify examples of onomatopoeia from those sports.
5. Give students time to draft poems that describe sporting events using onomatopoeia.

Sports Poems: Onomatopoeia (cont.)

6. Students should choose interesting phrases and arrange them—chronologically, top to bottom, left to right, etc.—to highlight aspects of the sports.

7. When they are finished with their drafts, students may add elements to highlight the visual impacts of their poems.

Onomatopoeia Words

bam	clap	kerplunk	splosh
bang	clip clop	lub dub	swish
bash	crunch	moan	thud
boing	cuckoo	pow	thump
boink	ding	rumble	ugh
bong	grunt	rush	whizz
bonk	guffaw	slap	whoop
boo	gurgle	snort	whoosh
boo-hoo	hack	splash	zing
bump	hiss	splish	zoom

Talking Back to Poems

Overview

Poets often use other poems to get ideas for their own writing. Students will develop ideas for their poems by drawing phrases and techniques from other poems to write their own work. By imitating a poem, writers can find powerful ideas for writing future poems.

Resources

- "What Other Families Eat for Lunch" by Ralph Fletcher
- "Being the Youngest" by Ralph Fletcher

Lesson

1. Read aloud a poem that speaks to you. Have students do the same with poems that speak to them.

2. Model for students how you underline interesting phrases, and comment on techniques that you notice in the text. Allow time for students to annotate their chosen poems.

3. Borrow something—a line, a word, or an idea from the poem. In the poem, "What Other Families Eat for Lunch," Ralph Fletcher laments the peanut butter and jelly he ate at home. In his other poem, "Being the Youngest," he talks about his place in the family.

4. Students may use these ideas to write "I am the oldest" poems or "I am an only child" poems.

5. Tell them to use the borrowed items to brainstorm more ideas for their poems.

BEING THE YOUNGEST

I'm eleven—youngest
one in the family.

There's Mom and Dad
plus my big brother,
God's gift to Girls.

He likes to call me
el bambino
and junk like that

but he's the oldest
so what would he know?

Nobody expects me
to act like an angel,
to be super polite.

Nobody's surprised if
I act spoiled, if I take
the last piece of cake

and that's the way
I like it.

—*Ralph Fletcher*

Talking Back to Poems (cont.)

6. Have students select the most interesting phrases and organize them into drafts. Then, encourage students to arrange the phrases to highlight central images. Consider adding some poetic techniques, such as onomatopoeia, simile, metaphor, and imagery, to add interest to the final versions.

WHAT OTHER FAMILIES EAT FOR LUNCH

For lunch Mom serves sandwiches: P-B-'n-J
or maybe grilled cheese with chowder,
or tuna fish with pickles and chips,
or, once, crabmeat sandwiches
but that was a special treat
I don't expect we'll
see again soon.

My friend Sal
invites me to his house.
They ask me to stay for lunch—
his mother serves steaming ravioli
a huge bowl of it plus garlic bread
so delicious I scarf down seconds and thirds
then she brings out this huge platter of cold cuts:
Pepperoni mortadella these cheeses I've never heard of

And the next day at home it's pretty hard going
back to Mom's P-B-'n-J sandwiches
with chips.

—*Ralph Fletcher*

WHEN WE TALK

When other families
talk at dinner,
they ask, "What
did you do
today?" They nod
and smile and
say things like,
"Good for you"

But we can't
sit still or
talk without raising
our voices and
our arms. We
find it so
outrageous that people
speak so softly—
when there is
so much wrong
with the world.

—*Chris Colderley*

Tanka

Overview

In this lesson, students learn about the tanka, a form of Japanese poetry that expands on the haiku form.

Resources

- Alexander, K. (2014). *The Crossover*. Houghton Mifflin Harcourt. "Tanka for Language Arts Class" (212).
- Alexander, K. (2007). *Crush: Love Poems*. Word of Mouth Books.

Lesson

1. Read a sample tanka, such as "Tanka for Language Arts Class" from page 212 in *The Crossover*.

2. Select the words and phrases that are connected to the senses.

3. Use the sensory words and phrases to describe the mood of the tanka.

4. Explain to students that a tanka follows this format:

    - Is 5 lines, 31 syllables (5, 7, 5, 7, 7)

    - Creates a mood with precise sensory words and phrases

    - Includes contemplation and reflection

    - Appeals to as many senses as possible

    - Is written in the present tense

5. Have students use the words and phrases to write sentences about their own chosen topics.

6. Tell them to cross out words that do not help to create clear images.

7. Work with students to write the sentences in five lines like a tanka. Have them count the syllables in each line. Allow time for them to play with the syllables and word choice to match the tanka form.

8. Publish your final copies.

Toys on Planet Earth Poems

Overview

Poets often use other poems to get ideas for their own writing. Students will develop ideas for their own poems about toys by remembering their favorite toys, as well as talking to some adults about their favorite toys.

Resource

"Toys on Planet Earth," in Nye, N. S. (2014). *A Maze Me: Poems for Girls*. Greenwillow Books.

Lesson

1. Read aloud the poem "Toys on Planet Earth" by Naomi Shihab Nye to students.

2. Discuss interesting phrases and comment on techniques that you notice in the text.

3. Ask students to make lists of their favorite toys (past or present) or look at the toy collection of a younger family member.

4. Have students use these ideas and observations to create lists of words and phrases to write their own toy poems.

5. Tell them to select the most interesting phrases and organize them into drafts.

6. Once they have completed their drafts, have them arrange the phrases to highlight central images. They should consider adding some poetic techniques, such as onomatopoeia, simile, metaphor, and imagery, to add interest to the final versions.

7. For the endings of their poems, they can borrow from Naomi Shihab Nye and their discussions with adults.

Writing Odes to Common Things

Overview

In "Ode to Pablo's Tennis Shoes," Gary Soto shows how important Pablo's tennis shoes are to him by highlighting details and making interesting comparisons. By using metaphors and similes, Soto makes readers understand just how these tennis shoes are very special.

Lesson

1. List a few everyday common things for which your students are grateful.

2. Have each student pick one of the common things and explain why it's important to them. Some examples for a pencil include the following:

    - can brainstorm with it
    - love to draw with it
    - able to build structures
    - love sharpening it
    - fun to take notes
    - tap it like a drumstick
    - able to use it as a javelin
    - write ideas and thoughts
    - write poems

3. Write similes and metaphors describing the object. For example, these could be used in comparisons about pencils:

    - a black paintbrush
    - a book in a stick
    - a cat's tongue on a stick
    - a craft stick
    - a pointy piece of graphite
    - a scriber of my ideas
    - a telephone pole for the train set
    - a thin drumstick
    - a thin orange mustache
    - a thin orange wand
    - a tree's grandson
    - a writing tree
    - a yellow dart
    - an arrow
    - lunch for a bored student
    - the top half of a rubber ball

4. Have students use the phrases to create their own odes!

Writing Odes to Common Things (cont.)

ODE TO PABLO'S TENNIS SHOES

They wait under Pablo's bed,
Rain-beaten, sun-beaten,
A scuff of green
At their tips
From when he fell
In the school yard.
He fell leaping for a football
That sailed his way.
But Pablo fell and got up,
Green on his shoes,
With the football
Out of reach.
Now it's night.
Pablo is in bed listening
To his mother laughing
To the Mexican *novelas* on TV.
His shoes, twin pets
That snuggle his toes,
Are under the bed.
He should have bathed,
But he didn't.
(Dirt rolls from his palm,
Blades of grass
Tumble from his hair.)

He wants to be
Like his shoes,
A little dirty
From the road,
A little worn
From racing to the drinking fountain
A hundred times in one day.
It takes water
To make him go,
And his shoes to get him
There. He loves his shoes,
Cloth like a sail,
Rubber like
A lifeboat on rough sea.
Pablo is tired,
Sinking into the mattress.
His eyes sting from
Grass and long words in books.
He needs eight hours
Of sleep
To cool his shoes,
The tongues hanging
Out, exhausted.

—*Gary Soto*

Team I: Editorial

Front Matter Template

Copyright Page

Written and Published by the Students of
School
Teacher's name
Principal's name
Address

in association with
Kwame Alexander's *The Write Thing*

Copyright by each individual author © Year

All rights reserved. No part of this book may be reproduced or transmitted in any form or by any means, electronic or mechanical, including photocopying, recording, or by an information storage and retrieval system, except by a reviewer who may quote brief passages in a review to be printed in a magazine or by a newspaper, without permission in writing from the publisher.

Table of Contents

Traditionally, a table of contents contains the name of each poem and the corresponding page number. You can certainly do that, but here's a much simpler way to do it, especially since this book is an anthology of many different students: List the names of the student authors in alphabetical order, with page numbers.

Student Authors and Publishers

Dedication

A formal, printed inscription in a book, piece of music, etc., dedicating it to a person, cause, or the like.

Foreword

A short introductory statement usually written by someone other than the author.

—Teacher or Principal, Title, Date

Introduction

A preliminary or beginning part of a book, leading up to the main part.

—Student Name, Grade

The Epigraph goes here:
An Epigraph is a relevant quotation at the beginning of a book, chapter, etc.

—Famous Person

Acknowledgments

An expression of thanks or a token of appreciation for those who helped in making the book possible or supported the project.

— Poetry participants in
The Write Thing
Writing Workshop

About Our School

Example: Wilcox Middle School, part of the Fenton County Public School District, is an innovative school serving seventh and eighth graders. It is full of dynamic, caring teachers and staff who collaborate and design creative lessons to help all students succeed. The diverse, multicultural student body brings a richness to the learning environment and to the school culture. Under the guidance of our principal, Wilcox Middle School is carving out new avenues of learning. It is in this positive climate that the chimes of learning can be heard ringing throughout the halls.

About the Students

Editorial Team
Willow is a fifth grader who enjoys reading, writing, art, and fashion.

Design Team
Thomas is a sixth grader who enjoys the color yellow and playing soccer.

Marketing Team
Polly is a third grader who likes history and wants to run for office someday.

Proofreading Team
Desiree is a fourth grader who enjoys writing stories about her travels.

Production Manager
Dawn is a seventh grader who loves school plays and listens to Lady Gaga.

Names: _____ Date:_____

Editorial Team Notes

Your group is responsible for writing and typing all the front and back matter and back cover copy. Pages 172–174 include templates to guide you through this process. It is also suggested that you look at other books in the library for information and inspiration. Everything you write and type should be proofread by the proofreading team.

Before you get started, please define the following:

Front Matter: _____

_____

Back Matter: _____

_____

Back Cover Copy: _____

_____

Back Cover Blurb: _____

_____

Tips

- The "About the School" section can be pulled from existing copy on the school's website or in the school's promotional materials. Ask your teacher where you might find this information if you have difficulty locating it.

- If your book will have sections, you need an epigraph to start each section. If your book will not have sections, you will only need one epigraph.

Team 1: Editorial

Editorial Checklist

Item to Complete	Who Is Assigned to Do This?	Completed	Proofread
Front Matter			
Copyright Page			
Table of Contents (Production manager is responsible for this).			
Subtitle			
Dedication			
Foreword			
Introduction			
Epigraph(s)			
Acknowledgments			
Back Matter			
About Our School			
About the Students (Production manager is responsible for this.)			
Back Cover			

(editorialchecklist.pdf)

Proofreading Checklist

When your book is printed, we don't want anyone to find any typos or erros (see, like that one). It is your group's responsibility to go through the manuscript and correct all errors. Please use a red pen.

To begin, follow these steps:

- Review the tips below and the *Proofreader's Marks and Symbols* (page 178).
- Read *Understanding How Grammar Works in Poetry* (page 179).
- Make sure the manuscript pages are numbered.
- *Note*: Other teams are writing new items for the book (e.g., Introduction). Please make sure that you have proofread all new work.

Here are your tasks for the day, in order of priority. Have fun!

Item to Complete	Who Is Assigned to Do This?	Completed	Ready to be Printed
Type all new poems			
Proofread all poems			
Proofread other teams' work			
Optional: Input all corrections into the word processing file.			

Tips and Things to Look For

- Every poem has a title.
- All pages, except blank pages, are numbered.
- Author names and titles are correct.
- There are no misspelled words.
- There are no missing words.

- All titles make sense.
- Periods and commas come before ending quotation marks.
- There are no extra spaces between words or letters.
- All the poems make sense.

(proofreadingchecklist.pdf)

Proofreader's Marks and Symbols

Use the following symbols to indicate your corrections.

Symbol	Definition	Sample
ℓ	delete something	take it way out
◡	close up space	print as o ne word
∧ or > or ∨	caret; insert something	insert here something
#	insert a space	insert here
stet	let stand; don't change it	let marked text stay as it is
¶	begin a new paragraph	
ⓢⓟ	spell out	change 5 lbs. to 5 pounds
≡	change to CAPITAL letters	make nato into NATO
Sm Cap or SC	use SMALL CAPITALS	change SIGNAL to SIGNAL
/	change to lowercase letters	make South into south
∿∿∿	use **boldface**	important should be **important**
⌃	insert a comma	for example insert a comma here
⌄	insert an apostrophe	Kwames book uses apostrophes
⊙	insert a period	Many sentences end with a period ⊙
—	italicize	make italics into *italics*

(proofreadingmarks.pdf)

Understanding How Grammar Works in Poetry

Do you want to write a **love poem**? Maybe you want to write a **silly poem** for a friend or even a pet? No matter what **type of poetry** you may be interested in writing, **grammar in poetry** is an important concept that deserves to be explored further.

First, understand that a **poem** is a compilation of words, but there is so much more than words. There is also how the words are used. Misspelling a word can have as much meaning as spelling the word properly. The same goes for **grammar in poetry**. Simply stated—the normal rules of grammar do not apply in **poetry**.

The **grammar in poetry** depends on the **beat**, the **meter**, and the **rhythm** of your own self. However, you have to show consistency. If you are going to **rhyme**, **rhyme** completely. If you are going to use fragmented sentences, use all fragmented sentences. If you are going to use single words, use single words throughout. If you use some punctuation, use correct punctuation through the whole **poem**.

Consistency in your grammar, no matter the style of grammar you use, will provide a piece of **poetry** that can be easily and smoothly read by your audience.

Grammar in poetry can determine a mood or a feeling. Saying "run" is going to mean more than "he ran." One is a passive feeling while the other is a more active feeling. If you are going to have a **love poem**, for instance, you may find a smooth pattern will have a more positive response than a jumpy or rough pattern. How you use your grammar will help the **poet** lead the direction of the target audience.

When you get stuck, investigate the benefits of reading other **poets** by visiting **PoetryAmerica.com**. You will discover there are many styles for you to choose from, and no single **poetry** or **poem style** is perfect for everyone or every occasion.

Grammar in poetry is probably as important as the spelling, and as long as there is a consistency, no one usage of grammar can be deemed inappropriate or appropriate. When you write any **poetry**, remember to do what feels right to you. There is no right or wrong in **poetry**, but the smoother a piece of **poetry** sounds, the more likely it will affect the readers.

Team 2: Proofreading

Team 3: Production

Production Manager Notes

Your job is to manage all the teams and make sure each one completes its tasks.

1. Find out who the team leaders are for each task. Explain to them that they will need to type and print everything out for you, as well as save everything in your Ready to Print folder or flash drive.

2. Research and define the following:

   Trim size: _____

   Paper color: _____

   Paper weight: _____

   Cover thickness: _____

   ISBN: _____

3. Generate a Table of Contents (see sample on page 172).

4. Start collecting biographies from each student. See the sample *About the Students* (page 174) and follow that same format.

5. Make sure you collect every file and get a printed copy of each team's work. Also, hand everything in to your teacher.

Tips

- You will be saving all files from each department in one location, such as on a flash drive. Guard the files with your life.

- You might want to keep digital and print copies of everything—just in case!

(productionmanager.pdf)

Production Checklist

Item to Complete	Staff Person	Completed	Proofread	Ready to Be Printed
Editorial				
Copyright Page				
Subtitle				
Dedication				
Foreword				
Introduction				
Epigraph(s)				
Acknowledgments				
About Our School				
Back Cover				
Marketing				
Book party plans				
Media alert for book launch				
Type name, contact, and email of local media for the press release				
Video blog				
Group photo				
Write blog				
Create flyer				

Team 3: Production

Team 3: Production

Production Checklist (cont.)

Item to Complete	Staff Person	Completed	Proofread	Ready to Be Printed
Design				
Choose cover template				
Look for photos				
Choose title font, color, and placement				
Choose cover colors				
Proofreading				
Type all new poems				
Proofread all poems				
Proofread other teams' work				
Production Managers				
Check in w/teams				
Printing spec sheet				
ISBN				
Library of Congress number				
Order bar code				
Everything ready to be printed				
Create TOC				
Write the About the Students				

(productionchecklist.pdf)

Marketing Checklist

In a few weeks, when your book comes back from the printer, you'll have a book party where you read from your book and sign copies for family and friends. To get as many people as possible to attend, you'll need to promote this book party. Your group will be in charge of all marketing and promotional aspects of the book party (media alerts, book party, signings, blogs, photography, video, etc.).

Please make note of the following steps:

1. Read the *Book Party Form* (page 185), and discuss what you'd like to do for your book party. After you fill in all information, discuss your ideas with your teacher to see if the dates and details work for the school.

2. Everything that you write/type today should be proofread by the proofreading team, then put it in the production manager's Ready to Print folder or save it to the flash drive.

3. Complete the checklist on page 184.

Tips

- Try to pick a time when your friends and families can attend your book party.

- Use social media to publicize your event!

- Talk to your teacher about providing snacks at your book party.

Marketing Checklist (cont.)

These are your tasks for the day, in order of priority:

Item to Complete	Staff Person	Completed	Proofread
Book party plans			
Media alert for book launch			
Type name, contact, and email of various local media so that you can send the press release (see example on page 186)			
Video blog: interview students about the workshop (*optional*)			
Coordinate a group photo			
Write a blog on the workshop (*optional*)			
Social media: one student can periodically post about the workshop			
Create a flyer to promote the book launch			

(marketingchecklist.pdf)

Book Party Form

Date: _____**Time:**_____

(Should be at least two months from now. Please check with your teacher to confirm date and location.)

Location: _____

Open to public or invitation only: _____ **Cost or free?** _____

How will you let people know about it? _____

Will there be food served? _____

Will this event need funding? If yes, where will it come from?

_____

What will be the program flow? *(Use back of this form.)*

Sample Program Flow

6:05	People arrive
6:15	Welcome by Johnny Rocket
6:17	Opening Remarks by Lenny Penny
6:19	Poets Perform
6:27	Special Guest Musician
6:30	Closing Remarks by Mrs. Obama
6:45	Students Sign Books

Team 4: Marketing

Sample Press Release

One School. Thirty Students. One Book.

Fifth graders from your school dedicated the fall semester to participating in Kwame Alexander's *The Write Thing* writing workshop. From start to finish, the students turned their poetry rough drafts into works of art. The library was turned into a publishing house where the cover was designed, the poems were proofread, and the foreword was written, all to produce the book called *I Am*. This book will be released on December 21 from 6:00–7:30 at the school library where poems will be presented, authors will autograph copies, and books will be sold.

For more information, contact:
Teacher, Your School at 555-555-5555 or Teacher@yourschool.edu

(pressrelease.pdf)

Video Checklist

At your book party, you may want to show a brief video on the workshop. The video will be comprised of interviews with students, teachers, and librarians. The following steps are your tasks:

1. Decide whether you will shoot your video on a phone, tablet, or with a video camera. Secure the device.

2. Choose a quiet location to hold interviews.

3. Decide who will record the interviews.

4. Decide who will be the interviewer.

5. Do a test interview before beginning.

6. Make sure everyone projects. **SPEAK LOUD**.

7. The following is the script that the interviewer could use.

   Interviewer: Please do not look at the camera. Direct all answers to me.

   Recorder: Press "Record."

   Interviewer: Please say and spell your name for the camera.

   Interviewer: (Choose any or all the following questions to ask each person):

   - *Why do you write?*

   - *What did you learn from the* Write Thing *writing workshop?*

   - *Do you have a favorite writer or poet? Why is that person your favorite?*

   - *What team were you on today?*

   - *Can you recite a poem for us today?*

❑ Choose video recording device.

❑ Find location.

❑ Choose person who will record video.

❑ Choose interviewer.

❑ Do a test interview.

❑ Practice speaking clearly and loudly.

❑ Brainstorm questions.

❑ Write script.

(videochecklist.pdf)

Design Checklist

Your group has the job of choosing the book's interior layout and coming up with a concept for the cover design. Here are some things to keep in mind:

1. Before you begin, please read *Guide to Book Cover Design* (page 189).

2. Please find four books in the library that have covers you really like. Explain to each team member why you chose them.

3. Find out what types of graphics programs (e.g., *Microsoft Publisher*, *Adobe Photoshop*, etc.) are on the computers in the school.

4. When you locate strong photos or illustrations, use the *Image Selection Form* (page 190) to keep track.

5. Feel free to sketch and draw your cover concepts as well.

These are your tasks for the day, in order of priority:

Item to Complete	Who Is Assigned to Do This?	Completed	Ready to be Printed
Brainstorm cover concepts			
Decide on the size of the book			
Research and select photos for cover			
Sketch and draw art for cover (*optional*)			
Choose colors for cover			
Choose title font, color, and placement			
Choose font and layout for the book's interior			

(designchecklist.pdf)

Guide to Book Cover Design

Like most people, you probably do judge a book by its cover. If the cover is unattractive, the chances of you buying it are highly unlikely. Deciding on the right colors, photos, and placement of text are all part of the design decision-making process. Who wants to buy the used gray bike in the dusty corner of the store when the brand-new, shiny, red 10-speed hangs in the window (on sale)? The design is the first element of your book that is solely customer-centric. If you build it (and it looks good), they will come.

Graphic design is the general term for artists who use computers to create and manipulate images and text to create some visual product. Whether it is a newspaper advertisement, letterhead, or a book cover, graphic designers spend endless hours coming up with visual ideas. Software programs that designers typically use include *Adobe InDesign*, *Corel Draw*, *Adobe Illustrator*, and *Adobe Photoshop*.

Choosing the right look for your cover is a challenging task. It must be a selling tool, so make it distinctive and intriguing to the eye. A cover that has vibrant colors will add a multi-dimensional effect, while a cover with black text on white projects nothing. Consider the use of artwork or photography on your cover. Depending on what you discover in your research, one may work better than the other. You can get images for your cover in a variety of ways. Choose a stock photograph or clip art.

Tips

- I highly recommend doing a lot of research! Look at hundreds of covers and book interiors. Find out what you like and what you don't like.

- Sketch what you want.

- Become familiar with the elements of good book cover design: color, images, and photographs.

Team 5: Design

(guidetobookcoverdesign.pdf)

Team 5: Design

Image Selection Form

Researching Your Cover Images

1. Search photos related to the theme and title of the book on a search engine and on stock photo and illustration websites, such as www.canstockphoto.com/ and www.istockphoto.com.

2. Type in keywords (related to your topic/theme) to start your search for images.

3. When you find images you like, there will be a number or file name under the pictures. Write it down on the image selection form. *Have fun!*

Website	Title of Image	Image ID #

(imageselection.pdf)

Guide to Interior Design

Choosing the Right Font for Your Book

Fonts are an important part of your book. They set the mood and can affect the readability of your text. Your book may be great, but if someone has trouble reading it due to a bad font choice, they may put it down without finishing or recommending it to a friend. Here are some common types of fonts and information on where they are suitable for use in your book.

Serif Fonts

Serif fonts are fonts that have a little line at the end of each stroke:

> Book Antiqua
> Bookman Old Style
> Garamond
> Times New Roman

Serif fonts may be used for every part of your book, such as the title, chapter titles, body text, or table of contents. Serif fonts are the easiest for reading large blocks of printed text. They should be the only type of font used for the main text of your book, such as your chapters.

Times New Roman was designed for use in newspaper printing presses in 1932 and is not ideal for use in a modern printed book. Consider selecting another serif font for your book.

Sans Serif Fonts

Sans serif fonts do not have a little line at the end of each stroke:

> Arial
> Calibri
> Tahoma
> Trebuchet MS
> Verdana

Team 5: Design

Guide to Interior Design (cont.)

Sans serif fonts are appropriate for the book title, chapter titles, headers, footers, subheadings, and any short lines of text but should NOT be used for the large blocks of text such as poems, the preface, or introduction. Sans serif fonts are not easily readable in printed large blocks of text. This is different from viewing text on a computer monitor. So even if you think your chapter text looks and reads fine in a sans serif font when viewing on your computer, be aware that the readability will be different when reading it in a printed book form. This has been tested and has been a long-held "rule" for book formatting.

Choosing a Page Layout

The term "page layout" is used to describe the way text and images are situated on a page. For your book to have a professional look and feel, there are a few basic principles to follow:

Contrast

In order for your page layout to be visually appealing and to keep the readers' interest, you should have contrast on your pages. Use a contrasting font for headings and titles, keeping the headings very different from the poem font. Don't go overboard—use one type for the poems and a different one for the titles. Consider a newspaper and how the headings are larger and bolder.

Alignment

Choose one justification and stick to it. As a rule, center justification will give the page layout a formal look. It is commonly used for wedding invitations, formal announcements, etc. Left justification will give your book a more professional look. Full justification within the layout will give your book a clean, orderly look. With full justification, your headings could be either left, right, or centered on the page.

Repetition

Create a sense of unity throughout your book by adding a few visual elements that you like, then repeat them throughout your book. Look through some of your favorite books to see what they have used on the pages; you may get some inspiration. Perhaps a decorative ornament under the heading of each chapter or a decorative drop cap to start each poem might give your book a special look.

(guidetointeriordesign.pdf)

Interior Layout Mini-Lesson

Overview

There are two elements of book design: cover and layout. This lesson is concerned with interior layout (also known as *page composition*). To ensure that our final book looks professional, is readable, and visually stands out, we must produce a creative masterpiece that entices readers. In this lesson, you will help students decide on a design for your poetry book's interior layout.

Objectives

- To use book publishing to inspire student writing.
- To introduce students to the challenge of page layout—how text and images work together with the page.

Resources

poetry books (from classroom or library)

Lesson

1. Have students view interior layouts of different poetry books and observe where page breaks occur, where the text is located on the page, and determine what style/size of text is used, and if and how images and other art are incorporated.

2. Discuss what students like and dislike about the various layouts.

3. Help students choose layout components for their book by answering the following questions:

    - What are the headers and footers, and where are they located (e.g., title, page numbering)?
    - What is the text font?
    - What is the text point size (e.g., 12 pt.)?
    - What is the line spacing (e.g., double-spaced)?
    - How is the text aligned (e.g., left justified)?

4. Work with students to discuss, try different layouts, and ultimately to select a layout for the book that is professional and appealing.

Solo Act Contributor Bios

Toni Blackman, artist and humanitarian, has traveled to more than 40 countries around the world. The first U.S. cultural ambassador for Hip Hop, she teaches workshops and gives talks for universities, conferences and festivals, corporations, and arts and religious institutions. Blackman signed a distribution deal with Independent Ear and is planning the release of an album and a content series of hip hop meditation music. She has shared the stage with the likes of Erykah Badu, Sheryl Crow, Yasiin Bey, Wyclef, The Roots, and Meshell Ndegeocello. Blackman's first book, *Inner-Course* (Random House/ Villard), was released in 2003. Her new book, *Wisdom of the Cypher*, has an anticipated 2019 release. Honored as a DOVE Real Woman, Blackman is a visiting scholar at New York University and in the teaching artist community at Carnegie Hall and the legendary Apollo Theater. (Solo Act on page 125)

Monica Burns, Ed.D., is an educational technology and curriculum consultant, author, and former New York City public school teacher. She visits schools across the country to support teachers to make technology integration meaningful and sustainable. Burns's website, ClassTechTips.com, helps educators focus on choosing "tasks before apps," promoting deep and purposeful learning with technology. (Solo Act on page 101)

Chris Colderley teaches elementary school in Burlington, Ontario. He is the coauthor of the *New York Times* bestseller, *Out of Wonder: Poems Celebrating Poets*. Colderley has conducted several workshops on teaching junior writers and using poetry in the classroom. He was awarded a Book-in-a-Day fellowship to study and write in Bahia. His articles and poems have appeared in *Inscribed: A Magazine for Writers*, *Möbius: The Poetry Magazine*, *Maple Tree Literary Supplement*, *TEACH* magazine, and *Language Magazine*. (Solo Act on page 88)

Tinesha Davis is a computer engineer, poet, and author of *Holler at the Moon: A Novel*. She serves on the board of directors of the Zora Neale Hurston/ Richard Wright Foundation and is a literacy coach for Book-in-a-Day. (Solo Act on page 109)

Solo Act Contributor Bios (cont.)

Arielle Eckstut and **David Henry Sterry** are cofounders of The Book Doctors. Eckstut is the author of nine books including *The Secret Language of Color: The Science, Nature, History, Culture and Beauty of Red, Orange, Yellow, Green, Blue & Violet*. She is also an agent-at-large at the Levine Greenberg Rostan Literary Agency, where for over 20 years, she has been helping hundreds of talented writers become published authors. Sterry is the author of 16 books on a wide variety of subjects, from memoir to middle-grade fiction, sports to reference. Their book, *The Essential Guide to Getting Your Book Published*, is the go-to book on the subject and takes you through the entire process of conceiving, writing, selling, marketing, and promoting a book. (Solo Act on pages 96–97)

Van G. Garrett is a middle school language arts teacher and an internationally celebrated artist and poet. His reviews and articles have appeared in *African American Review*, *Film and History: The Documentary Tradition* (CD-ROM), and *The Encyclopedia of African American History: 1896 to the Present*. His debut collection of poetry, *Songs in Blue Negritude*, is published by Xavier Review Press (2008). Garrett earned his MAIS degree from the University of Houston-Victoria and his undergraduate degree from Houston Baptist University. (Solo Act on page 123)

Marcelle Haddix is a dean's associate professor and chair of the Reading and Language Arts Center in the School of Education at Syracuse University. Her scholarly interests center on the experiences of students of color in literacy and English teaching and teacher education. She directs the Writing Our Lives project, a program geared toward supporting the writing practices of urban youth within and beyond school contexts. Haddix's work is featured in *Research in the Teaching of English*, *English Education*, *Linguistics and Education*, and *Journal of Adolescent and Adult Literacy*. She earned a Ph.D. from Boston College, a master's degree in education from Cardinal Stritch University, and a bachelor's degree in English education from Drake University. (Solo Act on page 33)

Solo Act Contributor Bios (cont.)

Kim Hardwick is a literacy advocate and principal of Clayton Huey Elementary School in New York. She has a bachelor's degree in literature from CUNY Bernard Baruch College, an MALS degree in education and SDA certification from SUNY Stony Brook. Hardwick has permanent New York State certification as a school district administrator and English teacher in Grades 7–12. (Solo Acts on pages 103 and 117)

Deanna Nikaido is a graduate from Art Center College of Design in Pasadena, California, with a degree in illustration and has authored two collections of poetry, *Voice Like Water* and *Vibrating with Silence* and a children's book, *Animal Ark*, co-authored with Kwame Alexander and Mary Rand Hess. She was the literacy coach and design specialist for Book-in-a-Day and worked as regional coordinator in northern and western Maryland for Poetry Out Loud, a national poetry recitation contest. (Solo Act on pages 16–17)

Ann Marie Stephens is the author of several picture books, including *Scuba Dog* and *Cy Makes a Friend*. She has been an elementary teacher for more than 26 years. She was a co-writer for *Trait Crate Plus* for grades 3 and 5, and she has had dozens of original ideas published in *Instructor* and *The Mailbox* magazines. Represented by Emily Mitchell at Wernick and Pratt Agency, Stephens is a seasoned presenter for both children and adults. She blogs for teachers: 2happyteachers.blogspot.com. Follow her on social media: Facebook (AMStephensAuthor) and Instagram and Twitter @AMStephens_. (Solo Act on pages 25, 40, 60, 66, and 91)

Marjory Wentworth's poems have been nominated for The Pushcart Prize six times. She is the author of four books of poetry and the children's book *Shackles*. Her most recent collaborations include *We Are Charleston: Tragedy and Triumph at Mother Emanuel* with Herb Frazier and Dr. Bernard Powers and *Out of Wonder: Poems Celebrating Poets* with Kwame Alexander and Chris Colderley. Wentworth teaches at The Art Institute of Charleston. She is the Poet Laureate of South Carolina. For further information please visit her website: www.marjorywentworth.net. (Solo Act on pages 26–27)

References

Alexander, K. (2002). *Do the write thing: 7 steps to publishing success.* Austin, TX: Manisy Willows Books.

Alexander, K. (2007). *Crush: Love poems.* Alexandria, VA: Word of Mouth Books.

Alexander, K. (2014). *The crossover.* Boston: Houghton Mifflin Harcourt.

Atwell, N. (1998). *In the middle: New understandings about reading, writing, and learning.* Portsmouth, NH: Heinemann.

Atwell, N. (2002). *Lessons that change writers.* Portsmouth, NH: Firsthand/Heinemann.

Beers, K. (2003). *When kids can't read: What teachers can do.* Portsmouth, NH. Heinemann.

Book-in-a-Day. (2011). *Hatching hope.* Alexandria, VA: Book-in-a-Day, Inc.

Calkins, L. M. (2001). *The art of teaching reading.* New York: Addison-Wesley Longman.

Calo, K. M. (2011). Comprehending, composing, and celebrating graphic poetry. *The Reading Teacher,* 64(5), 351–357.

Cecil, N. (1994). *For the love of language: Poetry for every learner.* Winnipeg: Peguis.

Certo, J. L. (2004). Cold plums and the old men in the water: Let children read and write "great" poetry. *The Reading Teacher,* 58(3), 266–271.

Certo, J. L., Apol, L., Wibbens, E., & Yoon, S. (2010). "Poetry writing PK–12: Current research and implications for practice and future research" in F. Troia, R. Shankland, and A. Heintz (Eds.), *Putting writing research into practice: Applications for teacher professional development.* New York: Guilford Press.

Cisneros, S. (2004). *Vintage Cisneros.* New York: Vintage Books.

Culham, R. (2013). *What principals need to know about teaching and learning writing, Second edition.* New York: Scholastic.

Eckstut, A., & Sterry, D. H. (2010). *The essential guide to getting your book published: How to write it, sell it, and market it ... successfully!* New York: Workman Publishing Company.

References (cont.)

Ediger, M. (2003). Exploring poetry: The reading and writing connection. *Journal of Instructional Psychology*, 30(2) 165–9.

Fletcher, R., & Portalupi, J. (2001). *Writing workshop: The essential guide*. Portsmouth, NH: Heinemann.

Frye, N. (2001). *Diaries of Northrup Frye*. Toronto, Canada: University of Toronto Press.

Haddix, M. (2011). Reclaiming and rebuilding the writer identities of black adolescent males. In D. Alvermann, K. Hinchman (Eds.), *Reconceptualizing the literacies in adolescents' lives: Bridging the everyday/academic divide, Third edition*. New York: Routledge.

Hale, C. (2013). *Sin and syntax: How to craft wicked good prose*. New York: Random House.

Heard, G. (1998). *Awakening the heart: Exploring poetry in elementary and middle school*. Portsmouth, NH: Heinemann.

Hirshfeld, J. (2010). Three keys: Opening the gate of poetry to young writers. *LEARNing Landscapes*, 4(1), 43–49.

Holbrook, S. (2005). *Practical poetry. A nonstandard approach to meeting content area standards*. Portsmouth, NH: Heinemann.

Janeczko, P. (2011). *Reading poetry in the middle grades: 20 poems and activities that meet the Common Core Standards and create a passion for poetry*. Portsmouth, NH: Heinemann.

Koch, K. (1990). *Rose, where did you get that red? Teaching great poetry to children*. New York: Vintage Books.

Kovalcik, B., & Certo, J. (2007). The poetry café is open! Teaching literary devices of sound in poetry writing. *The Reading Teacher*, 61(1), pp. 89–93.

Labbo, L. D. (2004). Poetry on the screen. *The Reading Teacher*, 58(3), 308–311.

Lansky, B. (2014). *How to write a haiku*. PoetryTeachers.com.

Linaberger, M. (2004). Poetry top 10: A foolproof formula for teaching poetry. *The Reading Teacher*, 58(4), 366–372.

References (cont.)

Marshall, J., & Newman, L. (1997). *Young adult literature: Exploration, evaluation and appreciation (3rd edition)* (252). Boston: Pearson Education.

McKeown, M., & Beck, I. L. (1999). Getting the discussion started. *Educational Leadership*, 57(3), 25–28.

McNeil, F. (1980). *When is a poem: Creative ideas for teaching poetry.* Collected from Canadian Poets. Toronto, Ontario: League of Canadian Poets.

Messner, K. (2001). Real revision: Authors' strategies to share with student writers. Portland, ME: Stenhouse.

National Commission on Writing In America's Schools and Colleges. (2003). "The Neglected 'R' The Need for a Writing Revolution." 10. April 2003.

Nelson, J. (2012). Digital poetry: New forms for an ancient art. Edutopia. www.edutopia.org/blog/digital-poetry-terry-heick

Neruda, P. (1994). *Odes to common things.* Boston: Little, Brown.

Ontario Ministry of Education. (2009). *Me read? And row! Ontario teachers report on how to improve boys' literacy skills.* Toronto, Ontario.

Palmer, E. (2014). Teaching the Common Core: The forgotten language arts. *Voices From the Middle*, 22(1), 73.22. No. 1, September, p. 73.

Parr, M., & Campbell, T. (2006). Poets in practice. *The Reading Teacher*, 60(1), 36–46.

Patel, P. (2014). Using formative assessment to improve presentation skills. *Voices From the Middle*, 22(1), 22–29.

Perfect, K. A. (1999). Rhyme and reason: Poetry for the heart and head. *The Reading Teacher*, 52, 728–737.

Portalupi, J., & Fletcher, R. (2005). *Teaching the qualities of effective writing.* Portsmouth, NH. Heinemann.

Ramirez, W. (2007). *Publication within a writing workshop as an effective strategy to increase student motivation, engagement and achievement in primary education.* Chico, CA: Chico State University.

References (cont.)

Redmond, G. (2012, October 31). *Exploring the imagistic turn in Jackie Earley's "One Thousand Nine-Hundred & Sixty-Eight Winters … "* voltagepoetry.com/editorial-team/

Reeves, D. B. (2002). *Accountability-based reforms should lead to better teaching and learning.* Harvard Education Letter.

Reeves, D. B. (2004). *Accountability for learning: How teachers and school leaders can take charge.* Alexandria, VA: ASCD.

Reeves, D. B. (2010). The write way. *American School Board Journal*, 197(11) 46–47.

Reid, L. (2006). From the editor. *English Journal*, 96(2), November 2006.

Routman, R. (2001). Everyone succeeds with poetry writing. *Instructor*, 111(1), 26–31.

Ruurs, M. (2010). Poetry inspired by poetry. *Reading Today*, 28(1), 46.

Sidman, J. (2007). *This is just to say: Poems of apology and forgiveness.* Boston: Houghton Mifflin.

Sweetland Center for Writing. nd. Using blogs in the classroom. University of Michigan Sweetland Center for Writing. lsa.umich.edu/sweetland/instructors/teaching-resources/using
-blogs-in-the-classroom.html

Tate, J. (2007). *Dream on. The best American poetry.* New York: Scribner.

Thinkmap visual thesaurus. www.visualthesaurus.com/

Tompkins, G, et al. (2002). *Language arts: Content and teaching strategies.* Toronto: Prentice Hall.

Williams, W. C., MacGowan, C., & Litz, A. W. (eds.) (1991). *The collected poems of William Carlos Williams, Vol. 1: 1909–1939.* New York: New Directions Publishing.

Wood, K. R. (2006). *Study-driven: A framework for planning units of study in the writing.* Portsmouth, NH: Heinemann.

Index

Index (cont.)

Index (cont.)

Index (cont.)

Index (cont.)

Index (cont.)

Digital Resources

Accessing the Digital Resources

The digital resources can be downloaded by following these steps:

1. Go to **www.tcmpub.com/digital**

2. Enter the ISBN, which is located on the back cover of the book, into the appropriate field on the website.

3. Respond to the prompts using the book to view your account and available digital content.

4. Choose the digital resources you would like to download. You can download all the files at once, or you can download a specific group of files.

ISBN:
9781493888429

Please note: Some files provided for download have large file sizes. Download times for these larger files will vary based on your download speed.

 ## Contents of the Digital Resources

- KwameTime videos (see page 19)

- example interior and exterior of a completed Book-in-a-Day manuscript

- student reproducibles

- copies of poems for shared reading opportunities

- KwameTime videos credit information

Credits

Text Credits

Kwame Alexander, "Picturing You," "Ten Reasons Why Fathers Cry at Night," and "When" from *And Then You Know: New and Selected Poems*. Copyright © 2012, 2009 by Kwame Alexander. Reprinted by permission of the author. Kwame Alexander, "Conversation After Lunch" from *Crush: Love Poems*. Copyright © 2007 by Kwame Alexander. Reprinted by permission of the author. Gwendolyn Brooks, "We Real Cool" from *The Bean Eaters*. Copyright © 1960 by Gwendolyn Brooks. Reprinted by permission of the Estate of Gwendolyn Brooks. Robert Burns, "A Red, Red Rose," 1794. Sandra Cisneros, "Cloud" from *Loose Woman*. Copyright © 1994 by Sandra Cisneros. Reprinted by permission of Random House, LLC. Jennifer Clement, "Lemon Tree" from *The Tree Is Older Than You Are*, translated by Consuelo de Aerenlund. Copyright © Jennifer Clement. Reprinted by permission of Simon & Schuster Books for Young Readers, a division of Simon & Schuster Children's Publishing Division. Mandy Coe, "For Those Who Don't Know What to Do With a Lake." Copyright © 2016 by Mandy Coe. Used by permission of the author. Chris Colderley, "What to Do With Blue," "Looking for a Morning Song," "If You Find a Book," "The White Chalk," "When We Talk," "Homework," and "Peanut Butter Jelly." Copyright © 2016 by Chris Colderley. Used by permission of the author. e. e. cummings, "2 shes" from *Etcetera: The Unpublished Poems*, edited by George James Firmage. Copyright © 1983 by the Trustees for the e. e. cummings Trust. Reprinted by permission of Liveright Publishing Corporation. Ralph Fletcher, "Being the Youngest," "What Other Families Eat for Lunch," and "Bedtime" from *Relatively Speaking: Poems About Family*. Copyright © 1999 by Ralph Fletcher. Reprinted by permission of Scholastic Inc. Nikki Giovanni, "And I Have You" from *Love Poems*. Copyright © 1968, 1970, 1971, 1972, 1974, 1975, 1978, 1979, 1983, 1995, 1996, 1997 by Nikki Giovanni. Reprinted by permission of HarperCollins Publishers, Inc. Kakinomoto no Hitomaro, "A Strange Old Man" from *100 Poems From the Japanese*, translated by Kenneth Rexroth. Copyright © 1976 by Kenneth Rexroth. Reprinted by permission of New Directions Publishing Corporation. Langston Hughes, "Harlem" from *The Collected Poems of Langston Hughes*. Copyright © 1994 by the Estate of Langston Hughes. Reprinted by permission of Random House, LLC. George Ella Lyon, "Where I'm From" from *Where I'm From: Where Poems Come From*. Copyright © 1999 by George Ella Lyon. Reprinted by permission of Absey & Company, Inc. Eve Merriam, "How to Eat a Poem" from *Jamboree: Rhymes for All Times*. Copyright © 1962, 1964, 1966, 1973, 1984 by Eve Merriam. Reprinted with the permission of Marian Reiner. Edgar Allan Poe, "The Raven," 1845. Alice Schertle, "Invitation From a Mole" from *A Lucky Thing*. Copyright © 1999, 1997 by Alice Schertle. Reprinted by permission of Houghton Mifflin Harcourt Publishing Company. Gary Soto, "Ode to Pablo's Tennis Shoes" from *Neighborhood Odes*. Copyright © 1992 by Gary Soto. Reprinted by permission of Houghton Mifflin Harcourt Publishing Company. William Carlos Williams, "The Red Wheelbarrow" and "This Is Just to Say" from *The Collected Poems: Volume I, 1909–1939*. Copyright © 1938 by William Carlos Williams. Reprinted by permission of New Directions Publishing Corporation. All rights reserved.

Photo Credits

front cover, p.9 Portia Wiggins; p.7 Lester Laminack; p.11 Album/Newscom; p.15, p.19, p.23, p.49, p.67, p.68, p.78, p.79, p.83, p.85, p.95, p.103 (bottom), p.104, p.108, p.113, p.115, p.117 (middle), p.121, p.122, p.131 Courtesy Kwame Alexander; p.16 Courtesy Deanna Nikaido; p.25, p.40, p.60 (top), p.66, p.91 Courtesy Ann Marie Stephens; p.26 Andrew Allen; p.30 Linda Holtslander; p.33 Courtesy Marcelle Haddix; p.88 Courtesy Chris Colderley; p.96 Courtesy Arielle Eckstut and David Henry Sterry; p.101 (top) Courtesy Monica Burns; p.103 (top), p.117 (top) Courtesy Kim Hardwick; p.123 Courtesy Van Garrett; p.125 Courtesy Toni Blackman; p.157 MM Photos/Shutterstock; all other images from iStock and/or Shutterstock.

Video Credits

Special thanks to students and staff of the following schools:
Clayton Huey Elementary School, Center Moriches, NY; Notably: Principal Kim Hardwick, Lori E. Damm Mellina, Colleen Hanzl, Dr. Thearl Barnard, and their fifth grade students; **Center Moriches Middle School**, Center Moriches, NY; Notably: Principal Melissa L. Bates and Allison Lesiewicz; **George C. Round Elementary School**, Manassas, VA; Notably: Principal Scott Baldwin, Ann Marie Stephens, and her first grade students
Video Production Team: Tinesha Davis, Kevin Carlson, Seed Multimedia LLC; Danny Miller, Production Editor/Copy Editor; Sarah Longhi, Editorial Director/Video Director; Brian LaRossa, Art Director; Sarah Morrow, Designer; Suzanne Akcelya, Assistant Editorial Manager; Danielle Bryant, Assistant Producer; Shelby Hast, Permissions Manager
Additional credits for the KwameTime videos are available in the digital resources (videocredits.pdf).